FREE Study Skills Videos/DVD Offer

Dear Customer,

Thank you for your purchase from Mometrix! We consider it an honor and a privilege that you have purchased our product and we want to ensure your satisfaction.

As part of our ongoing effort to meet the needs of test takers, we have developed a set of Study Skills Videos that we would like to give you for <u>FREE</u>. These videos cover our *best practices* for getting ready for your exam, from how to use our study materials to how to best prepare for the day of the test.

All that we ask is that you email us with feedback that would describe your experience so far with our product. Good, bad, or indifferent, we want to know what you think!

To get your FREE Study Skills Videos, you can use the **QR code** below, or send us an **email** at <u>studyvideos@mometrix.com</u> with *FREE VIDEOS* in the subject line and the following information in the body of the email:

- The name of the product you purchased.
- Your product rating on a scale of 1-5, with 5 being the highest rating.
- Your feedback. It can be long, short, or anything in between. We just want to know your impressions and experience so far with our product. (Good feedback might include how our study material met your needs and ways we might be able to make it even better. You could highlight features that you found helpful or features that you think we should add.)

If you have any questions or concerns, please don't hesitate to contact me directly.

Thanks again!

Sincerely,

Jay Willis
Vice President
<u>jay.willis@mometrix.com</u>
1-800-673-8175

SCAN HERE

CJBAT

Secrets Study Guide

CJBAT Practice Questions & Review
for The Florida Criminal Justice Basic
Abilities Test

Written and edited by Mometrix Test Prep

Printed in the United States of America

This paper meets the requirements of ANSI/NISO Z39.48-1992 (Permanence of Paper).

Mometrix offers volume discount pricing to institutions. For more information or a price quote, please contact our sales department at sales@mometrix.com or 888-248-1219.

Paperback
ISBN 13: 978-1-5167-0504-7
ISBN 10: 1-5167-0504-1

Ebook
ISBN 13: 978-1-5167-0886-4
ISBN 10: 1-5167-0886-5

DEAR FUTURE EXAM SUCCESS STORY

First of all, **THANK YOU** for purchasing Mometrix study materials!

Second, congratulations! You are one of the few determined test-takers who are committed to doing whatever it takes to excel on your exam. **You have come to the right place.** We developed these study materials with one goal in mind: to deliver you the information you need in a format that's concise and easy to use.

In addition to optimizing your guide for the content of the test, we've outlined our recommended steps for breaking down the preparation process into small, attainable goals so you can make sure you stay on track.

We've also analyzed the entire test-taking process, identifying the most common pitfalls and showing how you can overcome them and be ready for any curveball the test throws you.

Standardized testing is one of the biggest obstacles on your road to success, which only increases the importance of doing well in the high-pressure, high-stakes environment of test day. Your results on this test could have a significant impact on your future, and this guide provides the information and practical advice to help you achieve your full potential on test day.

Your success is our success

We would love to hear from you! If you would like to share the story of your exam success or if you have any questions or comments in regard to our products, please contact us at **800-673-8175** or **support@mometrix.com**.

Thanks again for your business and we wish you continued success!

Sincerely,
The Mometrix Test Preparation Team

TABLE OF CONTENTS

Introduction

Thank you for purchasing this resource! You have made the choice to prepare yourself for a test that could have a huge impact on your future, and this guide is designed to help you be fully ready for test day. Obviously, it's important to have a solid understanding of the test material, but you also need to be prepared for the unique environment and stressors of the test, so that you can perform to the best of your abilities.

For this purpose, the first section that appears in this guide is the **Secret Keys**. We've devoted countless hours to meticulously researching what works and what doesn't, and we've boiled down our findings to the five most impactful steps you can take to improve your performance on the test. We start at the beginning with study planning and move through the preparation process, all the way to the testing strategies that will help you get the most out of what you know when you're finally sitting in front of the test.

We recommend that you start preparing for your test as far in advance as possible. However, if you've bought this guide as a last-minute study resource and only have a few days before your test, we recommend that you skip over the first two Secret Keys since they address a long-term study plan.

If you struggle with **test anxiety**, we strongly encourage you to check out our recommendations for how you can overcome it. Test anxiety is a formidable foe, but it can be beaten, and we want to make sure you have the tools you need to defeat it.

1

Secret Key 1: Plan Big, Study Small

There's a lot riding on your performance. If you want to ace this test, you're going to need to keep your skills sharp and the material fresh in your mind. You need a plan that lets you review everything you need to know while still fitting in your schedule. We'll break this strategy down into three categories.

Information Organization

Start with the information you already have: the official test outline. From this, you can make a complete list of all the concepts you need to cover before the test. Organize these concepts into groups that can be studied together, and create a list of any related vocabulary you need to learn so you can brush up on any difficult terms. You'll want to keep this vocabulary list handy once you actually start studying since you may need to add to it along the way.

Time Management

Once you have your set of study concepts, decide how to spread them out over the time you have left before the test. Break your study plan into small, clear goals so you have a manageable task for each day and know exactly what you're doing. Then just focus on one small step at a time. When you manage your time this way, you don't need to spend hours at a time studying. Studying a small block of content for a short period each day helps you retain information better and avoid stressing over how much you have left to do. You can relax knowing that you have a plan to cover everything in time. In order for this strategy to be effective though, you have to start studying early and stick to your schedule. Avoid the exhaustion and futility that comes from last-minute cramming!

Study Environment

The environment you study in has a big impact on your learning. Studying in a coffee shop, while probably more enjoyable, is not likely to be as fruitful as studying in a quiet room. It's important to keep distractions to a minimum. You're only planning to study for a short block of time, so make the most of it. Don't pause to check your phone or get up to find a snack. It's also important to **avoid multitasking**. Research has consistently shown that multitasking will make your studying dramatically less effective. Your study area should also be comfortable and well-lit so you don't have the distraction of straining your eyes or sitting on an uncomfortable chair.

 The time of day you study is also important. You want to be rested and alert. Don't wait until just before bedtime. Study when you'll be most likely to comprehend and remember. Even better, if you know what time of day your test will be, set that time aside for study. That way your brain will be used to working on that subject at that specific time and you'll have a better chance of recalling information.

2

Finally, it can be helpful to team up with others who are studying for the same test. Your actual studying should be done in as isolated an environment as possible, but the work of organizing the information and setting up the study plan can be divided up. In between study sessions, you can discuss with your teammates the concepts that you're all studying and quiz each other on the details. Just be sure that your teammates are as serious about the test as you are. If you find that your study time is being replaced with social time, you might need to find a new team.

Secret Key 2: Make Your Studying Count

You're devoting a lot of time and effort to preparing for this test, so you want to be absolutely certain it will pay off. This means doing more than just reading the content and hoping you can remember it on test day. It's important to make every minute of study count. There are two main areas you can focus on to make your studying count.

Retention

It doesn't matter how much time you study if you can't remember the material. You need to make sure you are retaining the concepts. To check your retention of the information you're learning, try recalling it at later times with minimal prompting. Try carrying around flashcards and glance at one or two from time to time or ask a friend who's also studying for the test to quiz you.

To enhance your retention, look for ways to put the information into practice so that you can apply it rather than simply recalling it. If you're using the information in practical ways, it will be much easier to remember. Similarly, it helps to solidify a concept in your mind if you're not only reading it to yourself but also explaining it to someone else. Ask a friend to let you teach them about a concept you're a little shaky on (or speak aloud to an imaginary audience if necessary). As you try to summarize, define, give examples, and answer your friend's questions, you'll understand the concepts better and they will stay with you longer. Finally, step back for a big picture view and ask yourself how each piece of information fits with the whole subject. When you link the different concepts together and see them working together as a whole, it's easier to remember the individual components.

Finally, practice showing your work on any multi-step problems, even if you're just studying. Writing out each step you take to solve a problem will help solidify the process in your mind, and you'll be more likely to remember it during the test.

Modality

Modality simply refers to the means or method by which you study. Choosing a study modality that fits your own individual learning style is crucial. No two people learn best in exactly the same way, so it's important to know your strengths and use them to your advantage.

For example, if you learn best by visualization, focus on visualizing a concept in your mind and draw an image or a diagram. Try color-coding your notes, illustrating them, or creating symbols that will trigger your mind to recall a learned concept. If you learn best by hearing or discussing information, find a study partner who learns the same way or read aloud to yourself. Think about how to put the information in your own words. Imagine that you are giving a lecture on the topic and record yourself so you can listen to it later.

For any learning style, flashcards can be helpful. Organize the information so you can take advantage of spare moments to review. Underline key words or phrases. Use different colors for different categories. Mnemonic devices (such as creating a short list in which every item starts with the same letter) can also help with retention. Find what works best for you and use it to store the information in your mind most effectively and easily.

Secret Key 3: Practice the Right Way

Your success on test day depends not only on how many hours you put into preparing, but also on whether you prepared the right way. It's good to check along the way to see if your studying is paying off. One of the most effective ways to do this is by taking practice tests to evaluate your progress. Practice tests are useful because they show exactly where you need to improve. Every time you take a practice test, pay special attention to these three groups of questions:

- The questions you got wrong
- The questions you had to guess on, even if you guessed right
- The questions you found difficult or slow to work through

This will show you exactly what your weak areas are, and where you need to devote more study time. Ask yourself why each of these questions gave you trouble. Was it because you didn't understand the material? Was it because you didn't remember the vocabulary? Do you need more repetitions on this type of question to build speed and confidence? Dig into those questions and figure out how you can strengthen your weak areas as you go back to review the material.

 Additionally, many practice tests have a section explaining the answer choices. It can be tempting to read the explanation and think that you now have a good understanding of the concept. However, an explanation likely only covers part of the question's broader context. Even if the explanation makes perfect sense, **go back and investigate** every concept related to the question until you're positive you have a thorough understanding.

As you go along, keep in mind that the practice test is just that: practice. Memorizing these questions and answers will not be very helpful on the actual test because it is unlikely to have any of the same exact questions. If you only know the right answers to the sample questions, you won't be prepared for the real thing. **Study the concepts** until you understand them fully, and then you'll be able to answer any question that shows up on the test.

It's important to wait on the practice tests until you're ready. If you take a test on your first day of study, you may be overwhelmed by the amount of material covered and how much you need to learn. Work up to it gradually.

On test day, you'll need to be prepared for answering questions, managing your time, and using the test-taking strategies you've learned. It's a lot to balance, like a mental marathon that will have a big impact on your future. Like training for a marathon, you'll need to start slowly and work your way up. When test day arrives, you'll be ready.

Start with the strategies you've read in the first two Secret Keys—plan your course and study in the way that works best for you. If you have time, consider using multiple study

6

resources to get different approaches to the same concepts. It can be helpful to see difficult concepts from more than one angle. Then find a good source for practice tests. Many times, the test website will suggest potential study resources or provide sample tests.

Practice Test Strategy

If you're able to find at least three practice tests, we recommend this strategy:

UNTIMED AND OPEN-BOOK PRACTICE

Take the first test with no time constraints and with your notes and study guide handy. Take your time and focus on applying the strategies you've learned.

TIMED AND OPEN-BOOK PRACTICE

Take the second practice test open-book as well, but set a timer and practice pacing yourself to finish in time.

TIMED AND CLOSED-BOOK PRACTICE

Take any other practice tests as if it were test day. Set a timer and put away your study materials. Sit at a table or desk in a quiet room, imagine yourself at the testing center, and answer questions as quickly and accurately as possible.

Keep repeating timed and closed-book tests on a regular basis until you run out of practice tests or it's time for the actual test. Your mind will be ready for the schedule and stress of test day, and you'll be able to focus on recalling the material you've learned.

Secret Key 4: Pace Yourself

Once you're fully prepared for the material on the test, your biggest challenge on test day will be managing your time. Just knowing that the clock is ticking can make you panic even if you have plenty of time left. Work on pacing yourself so you can build confidence against the time constraints of the exam. Pacing is a difficult skill to master, especially in a high-pressure environment, so **practice is vital**.

Set time expectations for your pace based on how much time is available. For example, if a section has 60 questions and the time limit is 30 minutes, you know you have to average 30 seconds or less per question in order to answer them all. Although 30 seconds is the hard limit, set 25 seconds per question as your goal, so you reserve extra time to spend on harder questions. When you budget extra time for the harder questions, you no longer have any reason to stress when those questions take longer to answer.

Don't let this time expectation distract you from working through the test at a calm, steady pace, but keep it in mind so you don't spend too much time on any one question. Recognize that taking extra time on one question you don't understand may keep you from answering two that you do understand later in the test. If your time limit for a question is up and you're still not sure of the answer, mark it and move on, and come back to it later if the time and the test format allow. If the testing format doesn't allow you to return to earlier questions, just make an educated guess; then put it out of your mind and move on.

On the easier questions, be careful not to rush. It may seem wise to hurry through them so you have more time for the challenging ones, but it's not worth missing one if you know the concept and just didn't take the time to read the question fully. Work efficiently but make sure you understand the question and have looked at all of the answer choices, since more than one may seem right at first.

Even if you're paying attention to the time, you may find yourself a little behind at some point. You should speed up to get back on track, but do so wisely. Don't panic; just take a few seconds less on each question until you're caught up. Don't guess without thinking, but do look through the answer choices and eliminate any you know are wrong. If you can get down to two choices, it is often worthwhile to guess from those. Once you've chosen an answer, move on and don't dwell on any that you skipped or had to hurry through. If a question was taking too long, chances are it was one of the harder ones, so you weren't as likely to get it right anyway.

On the other hand, if you find yourself getting ahead of schedule, it may be beneficial to slow down a little. The more quickly you work, the more likely you are to make a careless mistake that will affect your score. You've budgeted time for each question, so don't be afraid to spend that time. Practice an efficient but careful pace to get the most out of the time you have.

Secret Key 5: Have a Plan for Guessing

When you're taking the test, you may find yourself stuck on a question. Some of the answer choices seem better than others, but you don't see the one answer choice that is obviously correct. What do you do?

The scenario described above is very common, yet most test takers have not effectively prepared for it. Developing and practicing a plan for guessing may be one of the single most effective uses of your time as you get ready for the exam.

In developing your plan for guessing, there are three questions to address:

- When should you start the guessing process?
- How should you narrow down the choices?
- Which answer should you choose?

When to Start the Guessing Process

Unless your plan for guessing is to select C every time (which, despite its merits, is not what we recommend), you need to leave yourself enough time to apply your answer elimination strategies. Since you have a limited amount of time for each question, that means that if you're going to give yourself the best shot at guessing correctly, you have to decide quickly whether or not you will guess.

Of course, the best-case scenario is that you don't have to guess at all, so first, see if you can answer the question based on your knowledge of the subject and basic reasoning skills. Focus on the key words in the question and try to jog your memory of related topics. Give yourself a chance to bring the knowledge to mind, but once you realize that you don't have (or you can't access) the knowledge you need to answer the question, it's time to start the guessing process.

It's almost always better to start the guessing process too early than too late. It only takes a few seconds to remember something and answer the question from knowledge. Carefully eliminating wrong answer choices takes longer. Plus, going through the process of eliminating answer choices can actually help jog your memory.

Summary: Start the guessing process as soon as you decide that you can't answer the question based on your knowledge.

9

How to Narrow Down the Choices

The next chapter in this book (**Test-Taking Strategies**) includes a wide range of strategies for how to approach questions and how to look for answer choices to eliminate. You will definitely want to read those carefully, practice them, and figure out which ones work best for you. Here though, we're going to address a mindset rather than a particular strategy.

Your odds of guessing an answer correctly depend on how many options you are choosing from.

Number of options left	5	4	3	2	1
Odds of guessing correctly	20%	25%	33%	50%	100%

You can see from this chart just how valuable it is to be able to eliminate incorrect answers and make an educated guess, but there are two things that many test takers do that cause them to miss out on the benefits of guessing:

- Accidentally eliminating the correct answer
- Selecting an answer based on an impression

We'll look at the first one here, and the second one in the next section.

To avoid accidentally eliminating the correct answer, we recommend a thought exercise called **the $5 challenge**. In this challenge, you only eliminate an answer choice from contention if you are willing to bet $5 on it being wrong. Why $5? Five dollars is a small but not insignificant amount of money. It's an amount you could afford to lose but wouldn't

want to throw away. And while losing $5 once might not hurt too much, doing it twenty times will set you back $100. In the same way, each small decision you make—eliminating a choice here, guessing on a question there—won't by itself impact your score very much, but when you put them all together, they can make a big difference. By holding each answer choice elimination decision to a higher standard, you can reduce the risk of accidentally eliminating the correct answer.

The $5 challenge can also be applied in a positive sense: If you are willing to bet $5 that an answer choice *is* correct, go ahead and mark it as correct.

Summary: Only eliminate an answer choice if you are willing to bet $5 that it is wrong.

Which Answer to Choose

You're taking the test. You've run into a hard question and decided you'll have to guess. You've eliminated all the answer choices you're willing to bet $5 on. Now you have to pick an answer. Why do we even need to talk about this? Why can't you just pick whichever one you feel like when the time comes?

The answer to these questions is that if you don't come into the test with a plan, you'll rely on your impression to select an answer choice, and if you do that, you risk falling into a trap. The test writers know that everyone who takes their test will be guessing on some of the questions, so they intentionally write wrong answer choices to seem plausible. You still have to pick an answer though, and if the wrong answer choices are designed to look right, how can you ever be sure that you're not falling for their trap? The best solution we've found to this dilemma is to take the decision out of your hands entirely. Here is the process we recommend:

Once you've eliminated any choices that you are confident (willing to bet $5) are wrong, select the first remaining choice as your answer.

Whether you choose to select the first remaining choice, the second, or the last, the important thing is that you use some preselected standard. Using this approach guarantees that you will not be enticed into selecting an answer choice that looks right, because you are not basing your decision on how the answer choices look.

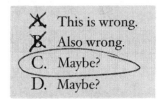

This is not meant to make you question your knowledge. Instead, it is to help you recognize the difference between your knowledge and your impressions. There's a huge difference between thinking an answer is right because of what you know, and thinking an answer is right because it looks or sounds like it should be right.

Summary: To ensure that your selection is appropriately random, make a predetermined selection from among all answer choices you have not eliminated.

Test-Taking Strategies

This section contains a list of test-taking strategies that you may find helpful as you work through the test. By taking what you know and applying logical thought, you can maximize your chances of answering any question correctly!

It is very important to realize that every question is different and every person is different: no single strategy will work on every question, and no single strategy will work for every person. That's why we've included all of them here, so you can try them out and determine which ones work best for different types of questions and which ones work best for you.

Question Strategies

⊘ READ CAREFULLY

Read the question and the answer choices carefully. Don't miss the question because you misread the terms. You have plenty of time to read each question thoroughly and make sure you understand what is being asked. Yet a happy medium must be attained, so don't waste too much time. You must read carefully and efficiently.

⊘ CONTEXTUAL CLUES

Look for contextual clues. If the question includes a word you are not familiar with, look at the immediate context for some indication of what the word might mean. Contextual clues can often give you all the information you need to decipher the meaning of an unfamiliar word. Even if you can't determine the meaning, you may be able to narrow down the possibilities enough to make a solid guess at the answer to the question.

⊘ PREFIXES

If you're having trouble with a word in the question or answer choices, try dissecting it. Take advantage of every clue that the word might include. Prefixes can be a huge help. Usually, they allow you to determine a basic meaning. *Pre-* means before, *post-* means after, *pro-* is positive, *de-* is negative. From prefixes, you can get an idea of the general meaning of the word and try to put it into context.

⊘ HEDGE WORDS

Watch out for critical hedge words, such as *likely, may, can, sometimes, often, almost, mostly, usually, generally, rarely,* and *sometimes.* Question writers insert these hedge phrases to cover every possibility. Often an answer choice will be wrong simply because it leaves no room for exception. Be on guard for answer choices that have definitive words such as *exactly* and *always.*

⊘ SWITCHBACK WORDS

Stay alert for *switchbacks*. These are the words and phrases frequently used to alert you to shifts in thought. The most common switchback words are *but*, *although*, and *however*. Others include *nevertheless*, *on the other hand*, *even though*, *while*, *in spite of*, *despite*, and *regardless of*. Switchback words are important to catch because they can change the direction of the question or an answer choice.

⊘ FACE VALUE

When in doubt, use common sense. Accept the situation in the problem at face value. Don't read too much into it. These problems will not require you to make wild assumptions. If you have to go beyond creativity and warp time or space in order to have an answer choice fit the question, then you should move on and consider the other answer choices. These are normal problems rooted in reality. The applicable relationship or explanation may not be readily apparent, but it is there for you to figure out. Use your common sense to interpret anything that isn't clear.

Answer Choice Strategies

⊘ ANSWER SELECTION

The most thorough way to pick an answer choice is to identify and eliminate wrong answers until only one is left, then confirm it is the correct answer. Sometimes an answer choice may immediately seem right, but be careful. The test writers will usually put more than one reasonable answer choice on each question, so take a second to read all of them and make sure that the other choices are not equally obvious. As long as you have time left, it is better to read every answer choice than to pick the first one that looks right without checking the others.

⊘ ANSWER CHOICE FAMILIES

An answer choice family consists of two (in rare cases, three) answer choices that are very similar in construction and cannot all be true at the same time. If you see two answer choices that are direct opposites or parallels, one of them is usually the correct answer. For instance, if one answer choice says that quantity x increases and another either says that quantity x decreases (opposite) or says that quantity y increases (parallel), then those answer choices would fall into the same family. An answer choice that doesn't match the construction of the answer choice family is more likely to be incorrect. Most questions will not have answer choice families, but when they do appear, you should be prepared to recognize them.

⊘ ELIMINATE ANSWERS

Eliminate answer choices as soon as you realize they are wrong, but make sure you consider all possibilities. If you are eliminating answer choices and realize that the last one you are left with is also wrong, don't panic. Start over and consider each choice again. There may be something you missed the first time that you will realize on the second pass.

⊘ AVOID FACT TRAPS

Don't be distracted by an answer choice that is factually true but doesn't answer the question. You are looking for the choice that answers the question. Stay focused on what the question is asking for so you don't accidentally pick an answer that is true but incorrect. Always go back to the question and make sure the answer choice you've selected actually answers the question and is not merely a true statement.

⊘ EXTREME STATEMENTS

In general, you should avoid answers that put forth extreme actions as standard practice or proclaim controversial ideas as established fact. An answer choice that states the "process should be used in certain situations, if…" is much more likely to be correct than one that states the "process should be discontinued completely." The first is a calm rational statement and doesn't even make a definitive, uncompromising stance, using a hedge word *if* to provide wiggle room, whereas the second choice is far more extreme.

⊘ BENCHMARK

As you read through the answer choices and you come across one that seems to answer the question well, mentally select that answer choice. This is not your final answer, but it's the one that will help you evaluate the other answer choices. The one that you selected is your benchmark or standard for judging each of the other answer choices. Every other answer choice must be compared to your benchmark. That choice is correct until proven otherwise by another answer choice beating it. If you find a better answer, then that one becomes your new benchmark. Once you've decided that no other choice answers the question as well as your benchmark, you have your final answer.

⊘ PREDICT THE ANSWER

Before you even start looking at the answer choices, it is often best to try to predict the answer. When you come up with the answer on your own, it is easier to avoid distractions and traps because you will know exactly what to look for. The right answer choice is unlikely to be word-for-word what you came up with, but it should be a close match. Even if you are confident that you have the right answer, you should still take the time to read each option before moving on.

General Strategies

⊘ TOUGH QUESTIONS

If you are stumped on a problem or it appears too hard or too difficult, don't waste time. Move on! Remember though, if you can quickly check for obviously incorrect answer choices, your chances of guessing correctly are greatly improved. Before you completely give up, at least try to knock out a couple of possible answers. Eliminate what you can and then guess at the remaining answer choices before moving on.

⊘ CHECK YOUR WORK

Since you will probably not know every term listed and the answer to every question, it is important that you get credit for the ones that you do know. Don't miss any questions through careless mistakes. If at all possible, try to take a second to look back over your answer selection and make sure you've selected the correct answer choice and haven't made a costly careless mistake (such as marking an answer choice that you didn't mean to mark). This quick double check should more than pay for itself in caught mistakes for the time it costs.

⌀ PACE YOURSELF

It's easy to be overwhelmed when you're looking at a page full of questions; your mind is confused and full of random thoughts, and the clock is ticking down faster than you would like. Calm down and maintain the pace that you have set for yourself. Especially as you get down to the last few minutes of the test, don't let the small numbers on the clock make you panic. As long as you are on track by monitoring your pace, you are guaranteed to have time for each question.

⌀ DON'T RUSH

It is very easy to make errors when you are in a hurry. Maintaining a fast pace in answering questions is pointless if it makes you miss questions that you would have gotten right otherwise. Test writers like to include distracting information and wrong answers that seem right. Taking a little extra time to avoid careless mistakes can make all the difference in your test score. Find a pace that allows you to be confident in the answers that you select.

⌀ KEEP MOVING

Panicking will not help you pass the test, so do your best to stay calm and keep moving. Taking deep breaths and going through the answer elimination steps you practiced can help to break through a stress barrier and keep your pace.

Final Notes

The combination of a solid foundation of content knowledge and the confidence that comes from practicing your plan for applying that knowledge is the key to maximizing your performance on test day. As your foundation of content knowledge is built up and strengthened, you'll find that the strategies included in this chapter become more and more effective in helping you quickly sift through the distractions and traps of the test to isolate the correct answer.

Now that you're preparing to move forward into the test content chapters of this book, be sure to keep your goal in mind. As you read, think about how you will be able to apply this information on the test. If you've already seen sample questions for the test and you have an idea of the question format and style, try to come up with questions of your own that you can answer based on what you're reading. This will give you valuable practice applying your knowledge in the same ways you can expect to on test day.

Good luck and good studying!

Test Overview

Law enforcement officer and corrections officer are two of the most important jobs in the United States, and they are also two of the noblest careers a person can aspire to. When we hear people talking about "public service" and "wanting to give something back to the community", they are usually politicians talking about their reasons for running for office. Politicians certainly play an important role in society, but a very strong argument can be made that no occupation even comes close to corrections officers and law enforcement officers in terms of giving back to the community and serving the public.

These two jobs are also rank very high on the list of the most difficult occupations, and not just physically. Yes, in order to work in corrections or law enforcement, a person certainly needs to be physically fit and prepared to deal with a violent attacker at a moment's notice, but the emotional and mental challenges of these jobs can be even more stressful over the course of a person's career. Most people have no idea how much sacrifice and dedication is required of a person who chooses to make this their life work. Law enforcement and corrections officers are truly the unsung heroes of our time.

Given how difficult these occupations are, and how little appreciation officers receive from society and the general public these days, it may come as a surprise to learn that competition for these jobs is stiff. If you hope to land one of these positions for yourself, it won't be easy, and you'll have to overcome many hurdles before you can join the ranks of the select few men and women in the front lines of corrections and law enforcement. One of the biggest challenges you'll face is making a good score on the Criminal Justice Basic Abilities Test, or CJBAT.

The state of Florida uses the CJBAT exam as a screening test for anyone seeking employment as a corrections officer (CO) or as a law enforcement officer (LEO). There are actually two different CJBAT exams—one is geared toward corrections officer positions, and the other is intended to be taken by people who seek careers in law enforcement. They are not interchangeable, so if a person changes career goals after passing the LEO form of the CJBAT, and decides that working as a corrections officer is a better fit, they will need to take the CO version of the CJBAT, and vice versa. It's important to note that a person can't enroll in a certified CO or LEO training program in the state of Florida without first achieving a passing score on the CJBAT.

The CJBAT is designed to ensure that anyone hired for a position in corrections or law enforcement possesses basic competency in three main areas which are important to fulfilling their duties—language, visualization, and reasoning. On the test, these areas are further broken down into eight specific sections: written comprehension, written expression, inductive reasoning, deductive reasoning, information ordering, spatial orientation, and memorization.

The CJBAT may sound intimidating, and the stress is heightened because so much is riding on a passing score. However, while you should definitely take the exam seriously, and prepare for it properly, there's no need to be overly anxious about it. Instead of worrying,

17

establish regular study sessions to review and prepare for the test. Thousands of people have passed the CJBAT, and with proper preparation, you can, too. This guide will help you achieve the highest CJBAT score you're capable of.

Written Comprehension

There are two sections of the CJBAT that focus on testing your language abilities. Of course, since the CJBAT is a written test, it's fair to say that you'll need good language skills in order to do well on every section of the exam. However, only two of the sections are specifically measuring your language skills. This section, Written Comprehension, is the first one. The other section that focuses on language skills is Written Expression. Judging from the titles alone, these two sections may sound as if they're measuring pretty much the same things.

In a way, that's true. Both of these sections on the CJBAT are testing the same kinds of things but from two different perspectives. In fact, the titles are somewhat confusing, and it would probably be easier to understand the differences between these two sections if the title of this section were changed from Written Comprehension to Reading Comprehension. That would actually be a more accurate title, because this section is actually testing your abilities to quickly and accurately interpret passages that you've read. So, if you have any trouble keeping these two sections distinct in your mind, just think of this one as Reading Comprehension instead of Written Comprehension.

What Are These Questions Testing?

Written Comprehension questions are measuring your ability to quickly grasp and retain important information in written passages.

The ability to quickly and accurately comprehend information expressed in a written form is critical to success in a law enforcement or corrections career. You'll regularly be reading training materials, letters, memorandums, laws, regulations, updates, policies, etc. Not all of these will be of equal importance, of course. Some will be less important, others will be critical, but all of them will have some level of importance. As a corrections or law enforcement officer, it will be imperative for you to understand everything you read. In these career fields, mistakes arising from poor reading comprehension skills can have devastating and far-reaching consequences.

What Is the Question Format?

The questions in Written Comprehension will share a similar format. You'll be given a reading passage, usually about one paragraph long. In most cases, there will be a lot going on in the passage. It may describe several different events, or it may feature a single event with several different people and/or items involved. Following the passage, one or more questions about it will be shown. In each one, you'll be asked about something you read in the passage. It will usually be some detail about a person or action described in the passage. What makes these questions so difficult is that the reading passages contain a lot of details, which means that it will be difficult to remember them all after a single reading, let alone keep them all separated. In other words, after you read each question, you'll usually need to go back and dig through the passage to find the right answer.

19

WHAT STRATEGIES OR TECHNIQUES CAN I USE TO DO WELL ON THIS SECTION?

In the Written Comprehension section, you'll need to balance two things—speed and accuracy. Ideally, you would be able to go at your own pace, and read as slowly as you need to in order to make sure your accuracy is perfect. However, you'll be up against a time limit, which means you can't necessarily take as much time as you'd like and read at a nice, leisurely pace, or you might run out of time and wind up not answering all the questions. In other words, you have a dilemma—if you go too fast, you risk making errors, but if you go too slowly, you risk not answering all the questions. Either one is bad and will result in a lower score. However, the test is designed so that the average person should have no trouble reading fast enough to answer all the questions, without sacrificing accuracy. Although it may sound trite, a key to success is to not worry about your speed when reading the passage. You should read at about the same pace you use in everyday reading.

Unless you have a lot of difficulty reading, answering these questions isn't all that complicated. The questions are pretty straightforward—who did what, where did an action take place, how many suspects were there, etc. However, the main reason people do poorly on this section is because there's usually quite a bit of information in each passage, and it's very easy to confuse one person or item or location for another, and select the wrong answer. To avoid this, a very effective strategy you can use is to read the question before reading the actual passage, so you know what you're looking for. Of course, you should also make certain you've read the question very carefully. If necessary and if you have time, read the question at least twice—once before you look for the answer in the passage, and again after you've selected an answer choice. For most people, the two steps of reading the questions before reading the passage, and then reading the question again after an answer has been chosen are probably the best way to of improving their chances of making a good score in Written Comprehension.

In addition to being relaxed and not stressing out over the questions, and making sure you understand each question, it's also important to practice ahead of time. This guide has many questions you can use for practice, but you don't need to stop there. Pick up a book or a magazine and read a brief passage from it that contains a lot of details. Then give the reading material to a friend or family member and have them quiz you over it to see how many details you can recall correctly. Do this on a regular basis, and use the practice questions in this book, and you'll be far better prepared for these questions than the average person taking the CJBAT. In addition, the peace of mind you'll have knowing that you're prepared will help you stay relaxed and focused on the test.

Practice Questions

1. At approximately 2:27 p.m. on Friday, Officer Naomi Jensen and Officer Kurt Sweitzer pulled over a 1992 Jeep Wrangler for a missing tail light. The female driver, who identified herself as Cindy Ortega, and the male passenger, who said his name was Jesse Ruiz, appeared to both officers to be acting in a suspicious manner, and neither one had any form of identification with them. The driver gave permission for a search of the vehicle, and in the trunk, officers discovered two purses and two wallets which appeared to be stolen from elderly people, and several expensive items which had recently been purchased, still in their bags. On questioning, Cindy Ortega admitted that the items had been purchased with stolen credit cards taken from the wallets and purses, which they had obtained from an associate who works in a nursing home.

Why did the officers pull the car over originally?
   A. Missing tail light
   B. Running a stop sign
   C. Failure to yield
   D. Speeding in a school zone

2. At 9:12 on the evening of July 23rd, officers of the West Side 2nd Division were dispatched to the 4400 block of Gina Dr to investigate a call about a reported domestic disturbance involving a gun. Officers Thelma Swihart and Vernon Fournier arrived at the scene and determined that there was a disturbance between the occupants of an apartment and several parties who showed up at the residence, and that the disturbance stemmed from a child custody dispute. Questioning revealed that the seven parties who showed up at the apartment illegally entered it, assaulting the occupants in the process, and threatened them with further harm, kidnapping, and death. The male occupant retrieved a handgun to defend himself but several of the suspects managed to wrest it from him. No shots were fired during the disturbance. The seven suspects who showed up at the residence were arrested for multiple charges including 1st Degree Burglary, Assault, Harassment, Battery, and Child Abuse. All seven parties were later booked into the El Paso County Criminal Justice Center on those charges.

How many officers were at the scene?
   A. Two
   B. Three
   C. Four
   D. Five

3. In early November, the police department began receiving calls about a man passing counterfeit currency at stores. On November 4, a pizza restaurant called the police and said that after closing they noticed that one of the $20 bills in the cash register looked funny. Officers determined that it was indeed a counterfeit bill. The store manager said no one there remembered who they got it from. The next day, police were called to a mobile phone store downtown, where the manager turned over twenty $20 bills a man had attempted to pay for a phone with. When the manager began scrutinizing the bills, the man fled the store. Officers got a good description of the man from the store personnel. On November 8, the same thing happened at another phone store, where a man matching the description fled the store after trying to pass $300 in phony $20 bills. On November 9, the man was finally captured when an off-duty officer happened to be in a jewelry store when the man tried to purchase a $2000 ring with counterfeit bills. When the store manager became suspicious, the man started to flee, but the off-duty officer was able to restrain him. A few minutes later, two officers arrived and arrested him on counterfeiting charges.

On which day did the man try to pass $400 in fake currency at a phone store?

    A. November 4
    B. November 5
    C. November 6
    D. November 8

4. On Sunday, May 18, approximately 17:19, two members of the police department responded to the vicinity of I-10 and 11th Avenue regarding a call from a motorist about shots being fired. Initial information provided by the caller indicated that an unknown suspect was shooting at cars while traveling on the interstate and that one of the bullets struck her back window. The caller advised that her husband and child were also in the vehicle with her. The caller said she could not provide any information about the suspect, or any reason anyone would want to shoot her. Officers were able to locate the caller's vehicle at the intersection of 11th Avenue and Gladys Street. The officers were able to verify that the rear window appeared to be shot out. The officers attempted to pull the car over but the driver, who turned out to be the husband of the caller, refused to pull over and a brief pursuit ensued. Officers were able to make contact with the occupants of the caller's vehicle when the driver finally pulled over at the intersection of 11th Avenue and College Street. During further investigation the officers learned that the callers, Heather Bates, was also the suspect, as she had actually fired several shots inside the vehicle in close proximity to her toddler child. The story that someone else had been shooting at the car turned out to be false. Heather Bates was booked into the Jefferson County Justice Center on the charges of Possession of a Weapon by a Previous Offender, Child Abuse, and Reckless Endangerment. Her husband, Steve Bates, was cited and released for Misdemeanor Vehicular Eluding and Child Abuse.

Where was the caller's car pulled over?
   A. I-10 and 11th Avenue
   B. I-10 and Gladys Street
   C. Gladys Street and College Street
   D. 11th Avenue and College Street

5. On May 2, at approximately 2:05 a.m., a caller reported there had been a road rage incident. The caller said the suspect pickup truck rammed the victim's car at the intersection of Calder Avenue and 8th Street, and then a male passenger in the truck had pointed a gun at the victim before fleeing the scene. As officers were on the way to the area, another call was received from a few blocks away, near the intersection of Calder Avenue and MLK Parkway. The caller stated that a pickup truck matching the suspect vehicle description was stopped in the middle of the street and several males had gotten out of the truck and were kicking it and smashing it with rocks. They then fled the area on foot and were not located. Officers determined that the truck from the road rage incident was a stolen vehicle that had not been reported stolen yet. It turned out that it had been stolen from a residence near the intersection of 9th Street and Hazel Avenue. The truck also contained property that had been stolen out of a different vehicle at a residence near the intersection of Ashley Avenue and 10th Street. No arrests have been made at this time; police describe the suspects as four white or Hispanic males in their early 20s.

The personal property was taken from a vehicle near the intersection of:

A. Calder Avenue and MLK Parkway
B. Calder Avenue and 8th Street
C. Ashley Avenue and 10th Street
D. 9th Street and Hazel Avenue

Practice Answers

1. A: Missing tail light. This is stated in the first sentence of the passage.

2. A: Two. Officers Thelma Swihart and Vernon Fournier were at the scene.

3. B: November 5. On the day after November 4, the suspect tried to pay for a phone with $400 worth of phony $20 bills.

4. D: 11th Avenue and College Street. Officers were able to make contact with the occupants of the caller's vehicle when the driver finally pulled over at the intersection of 11th Avenue and College Street.

5. C: Ashley Avenue and 10th Street. Calder and MLK is where the suspects were kicking and throwing rocks at the truck. Calder and 8th Street was the scene of the hit and run the truck was involved in. The truck had been stolen from a residence near the intersection of 9th Street and Hazel Avenue. The truck contained property that had been stolen out of a different vehicle at a residence near the intersection of Ashley Avenue and 10th Street.

Written Expression

The Written Expression section is the other part of the CJBAT that measures your language abilities. It's a counterpart to Written Comprehension. On this part of the exam, you'll be tested for your ability to express your thoughts to others in the written language, while using proper grammar and spelling. As an officer of corrections or law enforcement, you'll need to be able to communicate well. That doesn't mean that you'll be expected to sound like a Harvard professor, but you will be expected to speak and write in a way that demonstrates professionalism when dealing with the public, co-workers, superiors, etc. Many officers spend a good part of their workday writing reports and are expected to know how to spell correctly and use proper grammar.

WHAT IS THE QUESTION FORMAT?

The format of the questions in Written Expression is simple and straightforward. There are two kinds—spelling and grammar. In questions about spelling, you'll be shown a sentence in which one of the words has been spelled incorrectly. In the answer choices, you'll be shown four of the words from the sentence, three of which are spelled correctly, and you'll have to choose the one that is misspelled. In the second type of question, you'll be given a sentence with a blank representing a missing word. You'll be asked to choose which of the four answer choices should go in the blank.

WHAT STRATEGIES OR TECHNIQUES CAN I USE TO DO WELL ON THIS SECTION?

There are two things you can do that will really help you improve your potential score in this section. First, if you don't read on a regular basis, you should start doing so immediately, and do a little reading every day between now and when you take the CJBAT. It's impossible to memorize all the rules of grammar and spelling, and it's also unnecessary. We mostly learn good grammar from being exposed to it on a daily basis. However, most people don't use proper grammar when they speak, as the spoken word is much more casual than most written text. Of course, when it comes to spelling, the spoken word isn't much help. So, it's important to read a little bit every day.

Newspaper and magazine articles, either in print on online, are great for this. These kinds of publications use trained, professional writers, and they expect them to use proper grammar and correct spelling. They also have several editors who inspect the writer's text for mistakes in spelling and grammar before they allow it to be published. Reading this kind of material every day will increase your ability to tell the difference between good grammar and poor grammar.

Don't worry, to do well on the CJBAT, you don't need to be able to win a spelling bee, or know all the technical terms of grammar, such as dangling participle, past perfect tense, attributive adjective, subjective case, etc. But you do need to be able to know something's not right when you see it in print. Reading every day will help you improve a lot in this regard.

The second thing you can do is to review this chapter every day. In it, you'll find an easy to read, but pretty thorough, guide to grammar and spelling, covering the main things you'll need to know. You'll learn the main rules of spelling, as well as the exceptions to those rules. (Nearly all spelling rules have some exceptions.) We also show you the main components of good grammar, explain what they're all about, and give you the rules for using good grammar and understanding why something is either right or wrong. None of it is very complicated, and there's no reason you can't master it. The key is to study and review a little bit each day. As you do so, your skills and your confidence in your abilities will steadily increase, and you'll be ready for the CJBAT Written Expression section when test day arrives.

Grammar

SUBJECT-VERB AGREEMENT

Verbs must agree with their subjects in number. In other words, singular subjects need singular verbs. Plural subjects need plural verbs. Singular is for one person, place, or thing. Plural is for more than one person, place, or thing. Subjects and verbs must also agree in person: first, second, or third. The present tense ending -s is used on a verb if its subject is third person singular; otherwise, the verb takes no ending.

> **Review Video: Subject-Verb Agreement**
> Visit mometrix.com/academy and enter code: 479190

NUMBER AGREEMENT EXAMPLES:

Single Subject and Verb: *Dan calls home.*

(Dan is one person. So, the singular verb *calls* is needed.)

Plural Subject and Verb: *Dan and Bob call home.*

(More than one person needs the plural verb *call*.)

PERSON AGREEMENT EXAMPLES:

First Person: I *am* walking.

Second Person: You *are* walking.

Third Person: He *is* walking.

PROBLEMS WITH SUBJECT-VERB AGREEMENT

WORDS BETWEEN SUBJECT AND VERB

The joy of my life returns home tonight.

(**Singular Subject**: joy. **Singular Verb**: returns)

The phrase *of my life* does not influence the verb *returns*.

The question that still remains unanswered is "Who are you?"

(**Singular Subject**: question. **Singular Verb**: is)

Don't let the phrase *"that still remains…"* trouble you. The subject *questions* goes with *is.*

COMPOUND SUBJECTS

You and Jon are invited to come to my house.

(**Plural Subject**: You and Jon. **Plural Verb**: are)

The pencil and paper belong to me.

(**Plural Subject**: pencil and paper. **Plural Verb**: belong)

SUBJECTS JOINED BY OR AND NOR

Today or tomorrow is the day.

(**Subject**: Today / tomorrow. **Verb**: is)

Stan or Phil wants to read the book.

(**Subject**: Stan / Phil. **Verb**: wants)

Neither the books nor the *pen is* on the desk.

(**Subject**: Books / Pen. **Verb**: was)

Either the blanket or *pillows arrive* this afternoon.

(**Subject**: Blanket / Pillows. **Verb**: arrive)

Note: Singular subjects that are joined with the conjunction *or* need a singular verb. However, when one subject is singular and another is plural, you make the verb agree with the closer subject. The example about books and the pen has a singular verb because the pen (singular subject) is closer to the verb.

INDEFINITE PRONOUNS: EITHER, NEITHER, AND EACH

Is either of you ready for the game?

(**Singular Subject**: Either. **Singular Verb**: is)

Each man, woman, and child is unique.

(**Singular Subject**: Each. **Singular Verb**: is)

THE ADJECTIVE EVERY AND COMPOUNDS: EVERYBODY, EVERYONE, ANYBODY, ANYONE

Every day passes faster than the last.

(**Singular Subject**: Every day. **Singular Verb**: passes)

Anybody is welcome to bring a tent.

(**Singular Subject**: Anybody. **Singular Verb**: is)

Written Expression

COLLECTIVE NOUNS

The family eats at the restaurant every Friday night.

(The members of the family are one at the restaurant.)

The team are leaving for their homes after the game.

(The members of the team are leaving as individuals to go to their own homes.)

WHO, WHICH, AND THAT AS SUBJECT

This is the man who is helping me today.

He is a good man who serves others before himself.

This painting that is hung over the couch is very beautiful.

PLURAL FORM AND SINGULAR MEANING

Some nouns that are singular in meaning but plural in form: news, mathematics, physics, and economics

The news is coming on now.

Mathematics is my favorite class.

Some nouns that are plural in meaning: athletics, gymnastics, scissors, and pants

Do these pants come with a shirt?

The scissors are for my project.

Note: There are more nouns in plural form and are singular in meaning than plural in meaning. Look to your dictionary for help when you don't know about the meaning of a verb.

Addition, Multiplication, Subtraction, and Division are normally singular.

One plus one is two.

Three times three is nine.

> **Review Video: Nouns as Different Roles in a Sentence**
> Visit mometrix.com/academy and enter code: 653909

COMPLEMENTS

A complement is a noun, pronoun, or adjective that is used to give more information about the verb in the sentence.

DIRECT OBJECTS

A direct object is a noun that takes or receives the action of a verb. Remember: a complete sentence does not need a direct object. A sentence needs only a subject and a verb. When you are looking for a direct object, find the verb and ask *who* or *what*.

Example: I took the blanket. (Who or what did I take? *The blanket*)

Jane read books. (Who or what does Jane read? *Books*)

INDIRECT OBJECTS

An indirect object is a word or group of words that show how an action had an influence on someone or something. If there is an indirect object in a sentence, then you always have a direct object in the sentence. When you are looking for the indirect object, find the verb and ask *to/for whom or what*.

Examples: We taught the old dog a new trick.

(To/For Whom or What was taught? *The old dog*)

I gave them a math lesson.

(To/For Whom or What was given? *Them*)

> **Review Video: Direct and Indirect Objects**
> Visit mometrix.com/academy and enter code: 817385

Predicate Nouns are nouns that modify the subject and finish linking verbs.

Example: My father is a lawyer.

Father is the subject. Lawyer is the predicate noun.

Predicate Adjectives are adjectives that modify the subject and finish linking verbs.

Example: Your mother is patient.

Mother is the subject. Patient is the predicate adjective.

> **Review Video: Complete Predicate**
> Visit mometrix.com/academy and enter code: 293942

PRONOUN USAGE

Pronoun-antecedent agreement – The antecedent is the noun that has been replaced by a pronoun. A pronoun and the antecedent agree when they are singular or plural.

Singular agreement: *John* came into town, and *he* played for us.

(The word *He* replaces *John*.)

Plural agreement: *John and Rick* came into town, and *they* played for us.

(The word *They* replaces *John* and *Rick*.)

To know the correct pronoun for a compound subject, try each pronoun separately with the verb. Your knowledge of pronouns will tell you which one is correct.

Example: Bob and (I, me) will be going.

(Answer: Bob and I will be going.)

(1) *I will be going* or (2) *Me will be going*. The second choice cannot be correct because *me* is not used as a subject of a sentence. Instead, *me* is used as an object.

When a pronoun is used with a noun immediately following (as in "we boys"), try the sentence without the added noun.

Example: (We/Us) boys played football last year.

(Answer: We boys played football last year.)

(1) *We* played football last year or (2) *Us* played football last year. Again, the second choice cannot be correct because *us* is not used as a subject of a sentence. Instead, *us* is used as an object.

Review Video: <u>Pronoun Usage</u>
Visit mometrix.com/academy and enter code: 666500

Pronoun reference – A pronoun should point clearly to the antecedent. Here is how a pronoun reference can be unhelpful if it is not directly stated or puzzling.

Unhelpful: Ron and Jim went to the store, and he bought soda.

(Who bought soda? Ron or Jim?)

Helpful: Jim went to the store, and he bought soda.

(The sentence is clear. Jim bought the soda.)

Personal pronouns – Some pronouns change their form by their placement in a sentence. A pronoun that is a subject in a sentence comes in the subjective case. Pronouns that serve as objects appear in the objective case. Finally, the pronouns that are used as possessives appear in the possessive case.

Subjective case: *He* is coming to the show.

(The pronoun *He* is the subject of the sentence.)

Objective case: Josh drove *him* to the airport.

(The pronoun *him* is the object of the sentence.)

Possessive case: The flowers are *mine*.

(The pronoun *mine* shows ownership of the flowers.)

Who or whom – *Who*, a subjective-case pronoun, can be used as a subject. *Whom*, an objective case pronoun, can be used as an object. The words *who* and *whom* are common in subordinate clauses or in questions.

Subject: He knows who wants to come.

(*Who* is the subject of the verb *wants*.)

Object: He knows whom we want at the party.

(*Whom* is the object of *we want*.)

SENTENCE STRUCTURES

The four major types of sentence structure are:

1. Simple Sentences – Simple sentences have one independent clause with no subordinate clauses. A simple sentence can have compound elements (e.g., a compound subject or verb).

   Examples:

   Judy watered the lawn. (Singular Subject & Singular Predicate)
   Judy and Alan watered the lawn. (Compound Subject: Judy and Alan)

2. Compound Sentences – Compound sentences have two or more independent clauses with no dependent clauses. Usually, the independent clauses are joined with a comma and a coordinating conjunction, or they can be joined with a semicolon.

   Example:

   The time has come, and we are ready.
   I woke up at dawn; then I went outside to watch the sun rise.

3. Complex Sentences – A complex sentence has one independent clause and one or more dependent clauses.

   Examples:

   Although he had the flu, Harry went to work.
   Marcia got married after she finished college.

4. Compound-Complex Sentences – A compound-complex sentence has at least two independent clauses and at least one dependent clause.

   Examples:

   John is my friend who went to India, and he brought souvenirs for us.
   You may not know, but we heard the music that you played last night.

> **Review Video: Sentence Structure**
> Visit mometrix.com/academy and enter code: 700478
>
> **Review Video: Intro to Sentence Types**
> Visit mometrix.com/academy and enter code: 953367

Written Expression

SENTENCE FRAGMENTS

A part of a sentence should not be treated like a complete sentence. A sentence must be made of at least one independent clause. An independent clause has a subject and a verb. Remember that the independent clause can stand alone as a sentence. Some fragments are independent clauses that begin with a subordinating word (e.g., as, because, so, etc.). Other fragments may not have a subject, a verb, or both.

A sentence fragment can be repaired in several ways. One way is to put the fragment with a neighbor sentence. Another way is to be sure that punctuation is not needed. You can also turn the fragment into a sentence by adding any missing pieces. Sentence fragments are allowed for writers who want to show off their art. However, for your exam, sentence fragments are not allowed.

Fragment: Because he wanted to sail for Rome.

Correct: He dreamed of Europe because he wanted to sail for Rome.

DANGLING AND MISPLACED MODIFIERS
DANGLING MODIFIERS

A dangling modifier is a verbal phrase that does not have a clear connection to a word. A dangling modifier can also be a dependent clause (the subject and/or verb are not included) that does not have a clear connection to a word.

Examples:

Dangling: *Reading each magazine article*, the stories caught my attention.

Corrected: Reading each magazine article, *I* was entertained by the stories.

In this example, the word *stories* cannot be modified by *Reading each magazine article*. People can read, but stories cannot read. So, the pronoun *I* is needed for the modifying phrase *Reading each magazine article*.

Dangling: Since childhood, my grandparents have visited me for Christmas.

Corrected: Since childhood, I have been visited by my grandparents for Christmas.

In this example, the dependent adverb clause *Since childhood* cannot modify grandparents. So, the pronoun *I* is needed for the modifying adverb clause.

MISPLACED MODIFIERS

In some sentences, a modifier can be put in more than one place. However, you need to be sure that there is no confusion about which word is being explained or given more detail.

Incorrect: He read the book to a crowd that was filled with beautiful pictures.

Correct: He read the book that was filled with beautiful pictures to a crowd.

The crowd is not filled with pictures. The book is filled with pictures.

Incorrect: John only ate fruits and vegetables for two weeks.

Correct: John ate *only* fruits and vegetables for two weeks.

John may have done nothing else for two weeks but eat fruits and vegetables and sleep. However, it is reasonable to think that John had fruits and vegetables for his meals. Then, he continued to work on other things.

RUN-ON SENTENCES

Run-on sentences are independent clauses that have not been joined by a conjunction. When two or more independent clauses appear in one sentence, they must be joined in one of these ways:

1. Correction with a comma and a coordinating conjunction.
   Incorrect: I went on the trip and I had a good time.
   Correct: I went on the trip, and I had a good time.

2. Correction with a semicolon, a colon, or a dash. Used when independent clauses are closely related and their connection is clear without a coordinating conjunction.
   Incorrect: I went to the store and I bought some eggs.
   Correct: I went to the store; I bought some eggs.

3. Correction by separating sentences. This correction may be used when both independent clauses are long. Also, this can be used when one sentence is a question and one is not.
   Incorrect: The drive to New York takes ten hours it makes me very tired.
   Correct: The drive to New York takes ten hours. So, I become very tired.

4. Correction by changing parts of the sentence. One way is to turn one of the independent clauses into a phrase or subordinate clause.
   Incorrect: The drive to New York takes ten hours it makes me very tired.
   Correct: During the ten hour drive to New York, I become very tired.

Note: Normally, one of these choices will be a clear correction to a run-on sentence. The fourth way can be the best correction but needs the most work.

Spelling

RULES OF SPELLING
WORDS ENDING WITH A CONSONANT

Usually the final consonant is doubled on a word before adding a suffix. This is the rule for single syllable words, words ending with one consonant, and multi-syllable words with the last syllable accented. The following are examples:

- *beg* becomes *begging* (single syllable)
- *shop* becomes *shopped* (single syllable)
- *add* becomes *adding* (already ends in double consonant, do not add a third *d*)
- *deter* becomes *deterring* (multi-syllable, accent on last syllable)

- *regret* becomes *regrettable* (multi-syllable, accent on last syllable)
- *compost* becomes *composting* (do not add another *t* because the accent is on the first syllable)

WORDS ENDING WITH Y OR C

The general rule for words ending in *y* is to keep the *y* when adding a suffix if the *y* is preceded by a vowel. If the word ends in a consonant and *y* the *y* is changed to an *i* before the suffix is added (unless the suffix itself begins with *i*). The following are examples:

- *pay* becomes *paying* (keep the *y*)
- *bully* becomes *bullied* (change to *i*)
- *bully* becomes *bullying* (keep the *y* because the suffix is *–ing*)

If a word ends with *c* and the suffix begins with an *e, i,* or *y,* the letter *k* is usually added to the end of the word. The following are examples:

- panic becomes panicky
- mimic becomes mimicking

WORDS CONTAINING IE OR EI, AND/OR ENDING WITH E

Most words are spelled with an *i* before *e*, except when they follow the letter *c,* **or** sound like *a*. For example, the following words are spelled correctly according to these rules:

- piece, friend, believe (*i* before *e*)
- receive, ceiling, conceited (except after *c*)
- weight, neighborhood, veil (sounds like *a*)

To add a suffix to words ending with the letter *e*, first determine if the *e* is silent. If it is, the *e* will be kept if the added suffix begins with a consonant. If the suffix begins with a vowel, the *e* is dropped. The following are examples:

- *age* becomes *ageless* (keep the *e*)
- *age* becomes *aging* (drop the *e*)

An exception to this rule occurs when the word ends in *ce* or *ge* and the suffix *able* or *ous* is added; these words will retain the letter *e*. The following are examples:

- courage becomes courageous
- notice becomes noticeable

WORDS ENDING WITH ISE OR IZE

A small number of words end with *ise*. Most of the words in the English language with the same sound end in *ize*. The following are examples:

- advertise, advise, arise, chastise, circumcise, and comprise
- compromise, demise, despise, devise, disguise, enterprise, excise, and exercise
- franchise, improvise, incise, merchandise, premise, reprise, and revise
- supervise, surmise, surprise, and televise

35

Words that end with *ize* include the following:

- accessorize, agonize, authorize, and brutalize
- capitalize, caramelize, categorize, civilize, and demonize
- downsize, empathize, euthanize, idolize, and immunize
- legalize, metabolize, mobilize, organize, and ostracize
- plagiarize, privatize, utilize, and visualize

(Note that some words may technically be spelled with *ise*, especially in British English, but it is more common to use *ize*. Examples include *symbolize/symbolise,* and *baptize/baptise.*)

WORDS ENDING WITH CEED, SEDE, OR CEDE

There are only three words that end with *ceed* in the English language: *exceed, proceed,* and *succeed.* There is only one word that ends with *sede,* and that word is *supersede.* Many other words that sound like *sede* actually end with *cede.* The following are examples:

- concede, recede, precede, and supercede

WORDS ENDING IN ABLE OR IBLE

For words ending in *able* or *ible,* there are no hard and fast rules. The following are examples:

- adjustable, unbeatable, collectable, deliverable, and likeable
- edible, compatible, feasible, sensible, and credible

There are more words ending in *able* than *ible*; this is useful to know if guessing is necessary.

WORDS ENDING IN ANCE OR ENCE

The suffixes *ence, ency,* and *ent* are used in the following cases:

- the suffix is preceded by the letter *c* but sounds like *s* – *innocence*
- the suffix is preceded by the letter *g* but sounds like *j* – *intelligence, negligence*

The suffixes *ance, ancy,* and *ant* are used in the following cases:

- the suffix is preceded by the letter *c* but sounds like *k* – *significant, vacant*
- the suffix is preceded by the letter *g* with a hard sound – *elegant, extravagance*

If the suffix is preceded by other letters, there are no steadfast rules. For example: *finance, elegance,* and *defendant* use the letter *a,* while *respondent, competence,* and *excellent* use the letter *e.*

WORDS ENDING IN TION, SION, OR CIAN

Words ending in *tion, sion,* or *cian* all sound like *shun* or *zhun.* There are no rules for which ending is used for words. The following are examples:

- action, agitation, caution, fiction, nation, and motion
- admission, expression, mansion, permission, and television
- electrician, magician, musician, optician, and physician (note that these words tend to describe occupations)

WORDS WITH THE AI OR IA COMBINATION

When deciding if *ai* or *ia* is correct, the combination of *ai* usually sounds like one vowel sound, as in *Britain*, while the vowels in *ia* are pronounced separately, as in *guardian*. The following are examples:

- captain, certain, faint, hair, malaise, and praise (*ai* makes one sound)
- bacteria, beneficiary, diamond, humiliation, and nuptial (ia makes two sounds)

PLURAL FORMS OF NOUNS

NOUNS ENDING IN CH, SH, S, X, OR Z

When a noun ends in the letters *ch, sh, s, x,* or *z,* an *es* instead of a singular *s* is added to the end of the word to make it plural. The following are examples:

- church becomes churches
- bush becomes bushes
- bass becomes basses
- *mix* becomes *mixes*
- buzz becomes buzzes

This is the rule with proper names as well; the Ross family would become the Rosses.

NOUNS ENDING IN Y OR AY/EY/IY/OY/UY

If a noun ends with a consonant and y, the plural is formed by replacing the *y* with *ies*. For example, *fly* becomes *flies* and *puppy* becomes *puppies*. If a noun ends with a vowel and *y*, the plural is formed by adding an *s*. For example, *alley* becomes *alleys* and *boy* becomes *boys*.

NOUNS ENDING IN F OR FE

Most nouns ending in *f* or *fe* are pluralized by replacing the *f* with *v* and adding *es*. The following are examples:

- knife becomes knives; self becomes selves; wolf becomes wolves.

An exception to this rule is the word *roof; roof* becomes *roofs.*

Written Expression

NOUNS ENDING IN O

Most nouns ending with a consonant and *o* are pluralized by adding *es*. The following are examples:

- hero becomes heroes; tornado becomes tornadoes; potato becomes potatoes.

Most nouns ending with a vowel and *o* are pluralized by adding *s*. The following are examples:

- portfolio becomes portfolios; radio becomes radios; shoe becomes shoes.

An exception to these rules is seen with musical terms ending in *o*. These words are pluralized by adding *s* even if they end in a consonant and *o*. The following are examples: *soprano* becomes *sopranos; banjo* becomes *banjos; piano* becomes *pianos.*

EXCEPTIONS TO THE RULES OF PLURALS

Some words do not fall into any specific category for making the singular form plural. They are irregular. Certain words become plural by changing the vowels within the word. The following are examples:

- woman becomes women; goose becomes geese; foot becomes feet

Some words become completely different words in the plural form. The following are examples:

- mouse becomes mice; fungus becomes fungi; alumnus becomes alumni

Some words are the same in both the singular and plural forms. The following are examples:

- *Salmon, species,* and *deer* are all the same whether singular or plural.

Practice Questions

1. The police officer's manual can't cover every _____ situation; sometimes you'll just have to use your best judgment.

Which of these words would be the correct choice to fill in the blank?

    A. conceivable
    B. workable
    C. dependable
    D. reliable

2. Under no circumstances is it ever acceptable to wear a dirty or wrinkled uniform to work.

One word in the above sentence is misspelled. It is:

    A. circumstances
    B. acceptable
    C. wrinkled
    D. uniform

3. Officers must always be vigilant, as a tense situation can _____ suddenly.

Which of these words would be the correct choice to fill in the blank?

    A. apprehend
    B. escalate
    C. insinuate
    D. confabulate

4. The arguement between the two hostile inmates threatened to cause turmoil in the mess hall.

One word in the above sentence is misspelled. It is:

    A. arguement
    B. hostile
    C. threatened
    D. turmoil

5. If you always do the right thing, you never have to worry about a guilty _____.

Which of these words would be the correct choice to fill in the blank?

    A. conscious
    B. consciousness
    C. consensus
    D. conscience

Practice Answers

1. A: The word *conceivable* is the only choice for filling in the blank that makes any sense. Situations can't really be *workable, dependable,* or *reliable.* But they can be *conceivable,* which means something that can be thought of or imagined.

2. B: The word *acceptible* should be spelled *acceptable.* The other words are spelled correctly.

3. B: The word *escalate* is the only choice for filling in the blank that makes any sense. *Escalate* means to move fast, or quickly become worse. *Apprehend* means to catch. *Insinuate* means to hint at something bad without actually saying it. *Confabulate* means to make up stories that aren't true without being aware that you're doing so.

4. A: The word *arguement* should be spelled *argument.* The other words are spelled correctly.

5. D: The word *conscience* is the only choice for filling in the blank that makes any sense. *Conscience* refers to an inner sense of right and wrong; a person's views of the morality of his behavior. *Conscious* means aware of and responding to what's going on in the world, as opposed to unconscious (a person in a coma). *Consciousness* is simply the state of being conscious. *Consensus* means a kind of agreement between people.

Memorization

WHAT ARE THESE QUESTIONS TESTING?

Memorization has its own section on the CJBAT because it's a skill that's vital to this line of work. Corrections officers and law enforcement officers need to be able to quickly note important facts and details about situations, environments, written communications, etc. You must also be able to quickly recall this information, and do so accurately. The questions in this section of the CJBAT measure your abilities at being able to note and recall specific information when necessary.

In most cases, the information will be the sort of things you deal with every day—addresses, phone numbers, the make and model of a vehicle, names, faces, security codes, etc. Other information will be less common, but more important, such as a new assignment or a new shift. Some information will be critically important, possibly being the difference between life and death for you, another officer, or members of the general public—details of a suspect's description or vehicle, the number of customers and employees still inside a building during a hostage situation at a bank , the layout of a facility in a prison riot, etc.

WHAT IS THE QUESTION FORMAT?

On this section of the CJBAT, for each question, you will be shown a photo. You will be allowed to look at the picture for one minute, in order to memorize as many details as you can about what's shown in the photo. After one minute is up, you will no longer have access to the photo. Either it will disappear from your computer screen, or you will be required to turn the page in the test booklet. You will then have to answer some questions about the specific details in the photo, without being able to look at it.

WHAT STRATEGIES OR TECHNIQUES CAN I USE TO DO WELL ON THIS SECTION?

The most important thing you can do to prepare for this section of the test is practice, practice, practice. Until they're tested on it, most people have no idea how difficult it is to recall facts and details from a picture they just looked at if it's taken away from them. As you will no doubt learn firsthand when you start working on the practice questions in this guide, it's not easy to look at a picture and memorize every single detail in one minute. In fact, forget about memorizing every detail—while most people can recall a few details of the picture after it's taken away, for nearly everyone, for most people it's a huge challenge to remember more than just a few.

However, the good news is that this is a skill that you can improve with practice. Not only can you improve it, you can see huge improvements, and in a short span of time if you're diligent about working on this ability in the weeks leading up to your CJBAT test date. To practice this skill effectively, you'll need another person because it doesn't really do you much good if you're asking yourself the questions. So find a friend, a loved one, or someone who is also prepping for the CJBAT and ask them to help you in this area.

You'll have plenty of material to work with—pick up any newspaper or magazine and you'll find lots of pictures you can use for this exercise. There are also tens of millions of photos of all kinds of things on the internet. Choose a picture, study it for one minute, and then have your partner ask you some questions about the picture while you can't see it. Do this with several pictures each session. You'll be surprised at how much better you get, and how soon. But don't slack off, because this is an ability that you have to use regularly in order to maintain your skills. If you stop, you'll find that your memorization abilities quickly get worse. So practice on a regular basis, and do it right up until the day of your CJBAT exam.

Practice Questions

Study the picture for one minute. Then turn the page and answer some questions about the picture.

Example Photo

1. How many people are shown in the photo?

    A. 7

    B. 6

    C. 5

    D. 4

2. How many of the men are NOT wearing a tie?

    A. 1

    B. 2

    C. 3

    D. 4

3. One of the men is wearing a flower in his lapel. It is the man who is:

    A. First on the left

    B. Second from the left

    C. First on the right

    D. Second from the right

4. How many of the men are wearing either a vest or a jacket in addition to a shirt?

    A. 1

    B. 2

    C. 3

    D. 4

5. Two of the men are holding something in their right hand. One man is holding something in his left hand. What is this man holding in his left hand?

    A. A beverage in a bottle

    B. A smartphone

    C. A beverage in a glass

    D. A small plate of dessert

Practice Answers

1. C: There are five people in the photo.

2. A: Four of the five men are wearing a tie; one is not.

3. D: The second man from the right is wearing a flower in his lapel.

4. B: The first man on the left is wearing a vest; the second man from the right is wearing a jacket.

5. C: The first man on the right is holding a beverage in a glass in his left hand.

Memorization

Deductive Reasoning

WHAT ARE THESE QUESTIONS TESTING?

Possessing good reasoning abilities is a vital necessity for anyone seeking a career in corrections or law enforcement. Corrections officers and law enforcement officers must be able to reason logically in order to function effectively on the job, follow orders, keep themselves safe from harm, and protect the public, persons in custody, and clients of the correctional system. Having a well-developed set of reasoning abilities gives an officer the tools he or she needs to form correct conclusions and make wise decisions.

There are several kinds of reasoning, but nearly all of them fall into one of the two big categories of reasoning—inductive and deductive. The majority of the logic, or reasoning, people use is inductive. Inductive reasoning is basically pattern noticing. We see low-hanging dark clouds and hear thunder, and we decide that a storm is probably on the way. Why? Because hundreds of times in the past, throughout our entire lives, dark clouds and thunder have almost always been followed by a storm. Sometimes the storm blows over, but experience has taught us that when we see dark clouds and hear thunder, we should avoid outdoor activities. That is a classic example of inductive reasoning.

Deductive reasoning works the other way around. While inductive reasoning is from the bottom up, and uses lots of little facts to develop a general rule, deductive reasoning is top down, and relies on making decisions and judgments based on the general rule.

WHAT IS THE QUESTION FORMAT?

On this section of the CJBAT, you will be shown some written text, which will be some rules, laws, or regulations about a particular topic. Then you'll be presented with a situation, or scenario, and a question about how to apply the information you read to the scenario. Then you'll be shown several answer choices. Choosing the correct answer will require you to correctly interpret the information in the text and apply it to the scenario.

WHAT STRATEGIES OR TECHNIQUES CAN I USE TO DO WELL ON THIS SECTION?

Once again, the most important strategy you can use in this section is to take the time to thoroughly read the information in the first part of the question that explains the rule or regulation or law, and also do a thorough job of reading the scenario that calls for you to apply the information.

Don't worry about seeing any trick questions on the CJBAT Deductive Reasoning exam. All of the information will be simple and straightforward, and there won't be any "gray areas" or questions that could have more than one right answer. Each question will have only one correct answer, and it will be clear cut if you apply the information in the text properly.

Once you've read the scenario, you'll want to look for clues in the text that can help you rule out obviously wrong answers. Words like *never, always, don't, must, should, shouldn't*, etc., can help you rule out some answer choices. For example, if the text says "an officer must never do X", then any answer choice where the officer is shown doing X is clearly wrong.

Also, pay particular attention to words like *if, when, after, before*, etc., because these can provide strong clues to help you narrow down your answer if you still have two or three choices left after getting rid of answers that are obviously wrong.

You should have plenty of time to read the text and the scenario carefully, so try to avoid rushing. Many mistakes in this section can be avoided by simply reading carefully.

Practice Questions

Here are some rules from the Police Officer Manual for a large city. Breaking any of these rules can result in receiving disciplinary action, up to and including being fired:

Rule 25: Failure to inventory and process recovered property in conformance with Department orders.

Rule 27: Disseminating, releasing, altering, defacing or removing any Department record or information concerning police matters except as provided by Department orders.

Rule 28: Participating in any partisan political campaign or activity.

Rule 29: Associating or fraternizing with any person known to have been convicted of any felony or misdemeanor, either State or Federal, excluding traffic and municipal ordinance violations.

Rule 30: Discussing bail with a person who is in custody except by those specifically authorized to let to bond.

Rule 32: Giving an opinion as to fine or penalty.

Rule 34: Recommending any professional or commercial service.

Rule 37: Advising any person engaged in a professional or commercial service that such professional or commercial services may be needed.

Rule 41: Soliciting or accepting any gratuity, or soliciting or accepting a gift, present, reward, or other thing of value for any service rendered as a department member, or as a condition for the rendering of such service, or as a condition for not performing sworn duties.

1. You are a police officer who has sworn to follow the above rules. Your spouse is going to a fundraising event for a political campaign and is asking if you can come. You should:
    A. Attend without offering money or services to the campaign
    B. Request permission to attend from your superior officer
    C. Explain that you cannot attend the event
    D. Attend, because you will not be on duty

2. You are a police officer who has sworn to follow the above rules. You answer a call about a break-in at a jewelry shop. You arrive to find that the owner of the shop has pepper-sprayed the burglar. As you apprehend the suspect, the owner hands you a watch in thanks for your help. You return the watch with an explanation that you are not allowed to receive gifts. Have you broken rule 41 from the manual?
    A. Yes, the offer of the watch has invalidated your judgement
    B. No, because you have not accepted the gift, you have not broken the rule
    C. It depends on whether you feel the offer affected your decision to arrest the suspect
    D. Only if you must take the owner's word on the burglary

3. Which of the following would be cause for disciplinary action?
   A. Donating money to a political party
   B. Writing an anonymous letter to the press with details on a confidential case
   C. Joining a poker group with someone previously convicted for operating an unlicensed vehicle
   D. Receiving a housewarming gift when moving into a new neighborhood

Money Laundering:

(a) A person commits an offense if the person knowingly:

(1) acquires or maintains an interest in, conceals, possesses, transfers, or transports the proceeds of criminal activity

(2) conducts, supervises, or facilitates a transaction involving the proceeds of criminal activity

(3) invests, expends, or receives, or offers to invest, expend, or receive, the proceeds of criminal activity or funds that the person believes are the proceeds of criminal activity

(4) finances or invests or intends to finance or invest funds that the person believes are intended to further the commission of criminal activity

(a-1) Knowledge of the specific nature of the criminal activity giving rise to the proceeds is not required to establish a culpable mental state under this section.

(b) It is a defense to prosecution under this section that the person acted with intent to facilitate the lawful seizure, forfeiture, or disposition of funds or other legitimate law enforcement purpose pursuant to the laws of this state or the US

(c) It is a defense to prosecution under this section that the transaction was necessary to preserve a person's right to representation as guaranteed by the Sixth Amendment of the United States Constitution and by Article 1, Section 10, of the Texas Constitution or that the funds were received as bona fide legal fees by a licensed attorney and at the time of their receipt, the attorney did not have actual knowledge that the funds were derived from criminal activity.

(d) An offense under this section is:

(1) a state jail felony if the value of the funds is $2,500 or more but less than $30,000

(2) a felony of the third degree if the value of the funds is $30,000 or more but less than $150,000

(3) a felony of the second degree if the value of the funds is $150,000 or more but less than $300,000

(4) a felony of the first degree if the value of the funds is $300,000 or more

Deductive Reasoning

4. A jeweler is negotiating a deal for the sale of over $45,000 in precious stones and jewels. During the trade, the customer mentions in confidence that the money offered in payment has come from an unspecified illegal activity. The jeweler doesn't notify anyone of the fact and finishes the deal. Which of the following describes the jeweler's situation?

    A. Because the jeweler knowingly aided in a transaction with the proceeds of criminal activity, he has committed an offense.

    B. Because the jeweler has only performed his job in a normal fashion, he has not committed an offense.

    C. Because the jeweler has not received any abnormal benefit from the exchange, the jeweler has not committed an offense.

    D. Because the jeweler does not know what crime the customer has committed, the jeweler has not committed an offense.

5. Which of the following would be a second-degree felony?

    A. Investing $180,000 in stocks and bonds for a non-profit organization

    B. Selling a gold watch found on the street for $2,000

    C. Working with an offshore bank to move $350,000 into a more reputable and lawful bank account for an identity theft group

    D. Selling a house to a drug dealer for $200,000 in dirty money

Practice Answers

1. C: You should explain that you cannot attend the event. Rule 28 prohibits participating in a political fundraiser.

2. B: Because you have not accepted or solicited the gift, you have not broken rule 41.

3. B: Releasing information concerning police matters on confidential cases is prohibited by rule 27. Rule 28 does not prohibit donation of money to political parties. Rule 29 does not prohibit associating or fraternizing with a person known to be convicted of traffic and municipal ordinance violations. Rule 41 does not prohibit accepting gifts not associated with the performing of duties as a police officer.

4. A: The person has facilitated a transaction involving the proceeds of criminal activity which is prohibited under rule (2)(a). Guilt of money laundering does not depend on whether the suspect performs his job as normal, receives abnormal benefits, or knows the specific nature of the criminal activity giving rise to the proceeds.

5. D: Selling a house for $200,000 of dirty money is a felony of the second degree. Option C is also illegal, but would be a felony of the first degree. Options A and B are not felonies.

Deductive Reasoning

Inductive Reasoning

WHAT ARE THESE QUESTIONS TESTING?

Every day, every person on earth uses his or her reasoning abilities, and not just a couple of times a day. In fact, it's not a stretch to say that most of us spend a good part of our daily lives doing some sort of reasoning. Actually, it's so much a part of our lives that it's almost automatic—most of the time we're engaged in reasoning we're not even aware that we're doing it. We make decisions and form conclusions constantly by using our reasoning faculties, as we're getting ready for work, driving, all day at work, deciding where and what to eat, if we should take an umbrella, what to buy someone for their birthday, if we should go back in the house and get our umbrella, and countless other decisions and conclusions daily.

There are two main kinds of reasoning –deductive, and inductive. Most of the reasoning we use throughout the day is inductive. It's much more informal than deductive reasoning (deductive reasoning is the foundation of the scientific process). You can compare inductive reasoning to putting together a puzzle—you use little bits of pieces here and there, you notice patterns, you match up a piece with a slot, and you build the whole from individual pieces. That's inductive reasoning—working from individual, specific pieces of information to form a larger conclusion. (Deductive reason works the other way around.)

Of course, not everyone has the same ability to reason inductively, and a high level of ability in this area is a basic necessity for anyone seeking a career in corrections or law enforcement. You will use your inductive reasoning skills often, especially when it comes to investigating crimes or facility rules that have been violated. It's no exaggeration to say that these skills will be crucial to your success in law enforcement or corrections.

This section of the CJBAT will test your inductive reasoning abilities in this area to make sure you're ready to be trained for a position in these demanding fields.

WHAT IS THE QUESTION FORMAT?

On this section of the CJBAT, you will be shown a set of data that is displayed in a visual format, usually a table, pie graph, or bar graph. Then you'll answer a question which will require you to interpret the visual data and draw a conclusion based on it.

WHAT STRATEGIES OR TECHNIQUES CAN I USE TO DO WELL ON THIS SECTION?

As is the case with every section of the CJBAT, one of the most important strategies is reading carefully. Even though the information will be presented in visual form, there will be written text explaining what each element of the table, chart, or graph represents. It's very important that you take enough time to make sure you understand every element of the data you're looking at.

The next important strategy is to visually confirm your answer choice. That is, once you've looked at the table, graph, or chart, and you've read the question, and chosen your answer, it's very important that you go back to the visual data and double check your answer. Don't just choose an answer and go on to the next question. You should have plenty of time to

interpret the visual data, read the question, choose an answer, and go back and double check your answer. There's no need to rush through the questions.

Finally, even if you've spent some time interpreting table, graphs, and charts, as many people do in their high school and college classes, it's important to brush up on your visual data interpretation skills, especially if you've been out of school for a while. If your classes didn't cover table, graph, and chart reading, it's even more important for you to get some practice in this area. We've included practice questions that can help you get better at interpreting visual data. Be sure to take advantage of these questions, as they are powerful tools for improving your skills in this area. In addition, make a regular habit of studying charts and graphs. Do it daily, if possible. Table, graphs, and charts are all around you. You'll find them on thousands of websites, or if you prefer, you can just head to your local library and start browsing through magazines. Most magazines have at least one or two such items in each issue, and there are hundreds of issues available at the typical public library.

Displaying Information

FREQUENCY TABLES

Frequency tables show how frequently each unique value appears in a set. A **relative frequency table** is one that shows the proportions of each unique value compared to the entire set. Relative frequencies are given as percentages; however, the total percent for a relative frequency table will not necessarily equal 100 percent due to rounding. An example of a frequency table with relative frequencies is below.

Favorite Color	Frequency	Relative Frequency
Blue	4	13%
Red	7	22%
Green	3	9%
Purple	6	19%
Cyan	12	38%

> **Review Video: Data Interpretation of Graphs**
> Visit mometrix.com/academy and enter code: 200439

CIRCLE GRAPHS

Circle graphs, also known as *pie charts*, provide a visual depiction of the relationship of each type of data compared to the whole set of data. The circle graph is divided into sections by drawing radii to create central angles whose percentage of the circle is equal to the individual data's percentage of the whole set. Each 1% of data is equal to 3.6° in the circle graph. Therefore, data represented by a 90° section of the circle graph makes up 25% of the whole. When complete, a circle graph often looks like a pie cut into uneven wedges. The pie chart below shows the data from the frequency table referenced earlier where people were asked their favorite color.

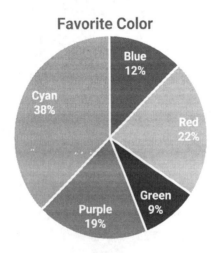

Favorite Color

PICTOGRAPHS

A **pictograph** is a graph, generally in the horizontal orientation, that uses pictures or symbols to represent the data. Each pictograph must have a key that defines the picture or symbol and gives the quantity each picture or symbol represents. Pictures or symbols on a pictograph are not always shown as whole elements. In this case, the fraction of the picture or symbol shown represents the same fraction of the quantity a whole picture or symbol stands for. For example, a row with $3\frac{1}{2}$ ears of corn, where each ear of corn represents 100 stalks of corn in a field, would equal $3\frac{1}{2} \times 100 = 350$ stalks of corn in the field.

Name	Number of ears of corn eaten	Field	Number of stalks of corn
Michael	🌽🌽🌽🌽🌽	Field 1	🌽🌽🌽🌽🌽
Tara	🌽🌽	Field 2	🌽🌽🌽
John	🌽🌽🌽🌽	Field 3	🌽🌽🌽🌽
Sara	🌽	Field 4	🌽
Jacob	🌽🌽🌽	Field 5	🌽🌽🌽🌽

Each 🌽 represents 1 ear of corn eaten.   Each 🌽 represents 100 stalks of corn.

Review Video: Pictographs
Visit mometrix.com/academy and enter code: 147860

LINE GRAPHS

Line graphs have one or more lines of varying styles (solid or broken) to show the different values for a set of data. The individual data are represented as ordered pairs, much like on a Cartesian plane. In this case, the x- and y-axes are defined in terms of their units, such as dollars or time. The individual plotted points are joined by line segments to show whether the value of the data is increasing (line sloping upward), decreasing (line sloping downward), or staying the same (horizontal line). Multiple sets of data can be graphed on the same line graph to give an easy visual comparison. An example of this would be graphing achievement test scores for different groups of students over the same time period to see which group had the greatest increase or decrease in performance from year to year (as shown below).

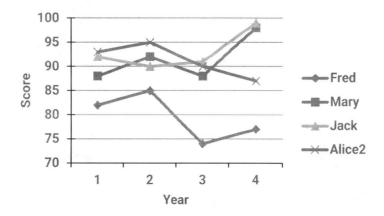

LINE PLOTS

A **line plot**, also known as a *dot plot*, has plotted points that are not connected by line segments. In this graph, the horizontal axis lists the different possible values for the data, and the vertical axis lists the number of times the individual value occurs. A single dot is graphed for each value to show the number of times it occurs. This graph is more closely related to a bar graph than a line graph. Do not connect the dots in a line plot or it will misrepresent the data.

STEM AND LEAF PLOTS

A **stem and leaf plot** is useful for depicting groups of data that fall into a range of values. Each piece of data is separated into two parts: the first, or left, part is called the stem; the second, or right, part is called the leaf. Each stem is listed in a column from smallest to largest. Each leaf that has the common stem is listed in that stem's row from smallest to largest. For example, in a set of two-digit numbers, the digit in the tens place is the stem, and the digit in the ones place is the leaf. With a stem and leaf plot, you can easily see which subset of numbers (10s, 20s, 30s, etc.) is the largest. This information is also readily available by looking at a histogram, but a stem and leaf plot also allows you to look closer and see exactly which values fall in that range. Using a sample set of test scores

$(82, 88, 92, 93, 85, 90, 92, 95, 74, 88, 90, 91, 78, 87, 98, 99)$, we can assemble a stem and leaf plot like the one below.

Test Scores

7	4	8						
8	2	5	7	8	8			
9	0	0	1	2	2	3	5	8	9

> **Review Video: Stem and Leaf Plots**
> Visit mometrix.com/academy and enter code: 302339

BAR GRAPHS

A **bar graph** is one of the few graphs that can be drawn correctly in two different configurations – both horizontally and vertically. A bar graph is similar to a line plot in the way the data is organized on the graph. Both axes must have their categories defined for the graph to be useful. Rather than placing a single dot to mark the point of the data's value, a bar, or thick line, is drawn from zero to the exact value of the data, whether it is a number, percentage, or other numerical value. Longer bar lengths correspond to greater data values. To read a bar graph, read the labels for the axes to find the units being reported. Then, look where the bars end in relation to the scale given on the corresponding axis and determine the associated value.

The bar chart below represents the responses from our favorite-color survey.

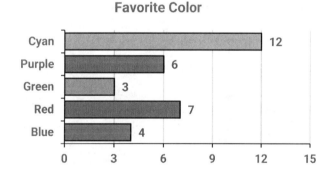

HISTOGRAMS

At first glance, a **histogram** looks like a vertical bar graph. The difference is that a bar graph has a separate bar for each piece of data and a histogram has one continuous bar for each *range* of data. For example, a histogram may have one bar for the range 0–9, one bar for 10–19, etc. While a bar graph has numerical values on one axis, a histogram has numerical values on both axes. Each range is of equal size, and they are ordered left to right from lowest to highest. The height of each column on a histogram represents the number of data values within that range. Like a stem and leaf plot, a histogram makes it easy to glance at the graph and quickly determine which range has the greatest quantity of values. A simple example of a histogram is below.

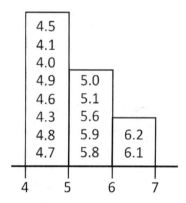

5-NUMBER SUMMARY

The **5-number summary** of a set of data gives a very informative picture of the set. The five numbers in the summary include the minimum value, maximum value, and the three quartiles. This information gives the reader the range and median of the set, as well as an indication of how the data is spread about the median.

BOX AND WHISKER PLOTS

A **box-and-whiskers plot** is a graphical representation of the 5-number summary. To draw a box-and-whiskers plot, plot the points of the 5-number summary on a number line. Draw a box whose ends are through the points for the first and third quartiles. Draw a vertical line in the box through the median to divide the box in half. Draw a line segment from the first quartile point to the minimum value, and from the third quartile point to the maximum value.

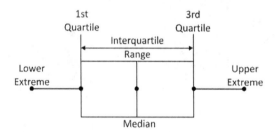

Review Video: **Box and Whisker Plots**
Visit mometrix.com/academy and enter code: 810817

EXAMPLE

Given the following data (32, 28, 29, 26, 35, 27, 30, 31, 27, 32), we first sort it into numerical order: 26, 27, 27, 28, 29, 30, 31, 32, 32, 35. We can then find the median. Since there are ten values, we take the average of the 5th and 6th values to get 29.5. We find the lower quartile by taking the median of the data smaller than the median. Since there are five values, we take the 3rd value, which is 27. We find the upper quartile by taking the median of the data larger than the overall median, which is 32. Finally, we note our minimum and maximum, which are simply the smallest and largest values in the set: 26 and 35, respectively. Now we can create our box plot:

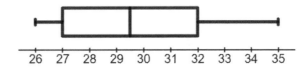

This plot is fairly "long" on the right whisker, showing one or more unusually high values (but not quite outliers). The other quartiles are similar in length, showing a fairly even distribution of data.

INTERQUARTILE RANGE

The **interquartile range, or IQR**, is the difference between the upper and lower quartiles. It measures how the data is dispersed: a high IQR means that the data is more spread out, while a low IQR means that the data is clustered more tightly around the median. To find the IQR, subtract the lower quartile value (Q_1) from the upper quartile value (Q_3).

EXAMPLE

To find the upper and lower quartiles, we first find the median and then take the median of all values above it and all values below it. In the following data set (16, 18, 13, 24, 16, 51, 32, 21, 27, 39), we first rearrange the values in numerical order: 13, 16, 16, 18, 21, 24, 27, 32, 39, 51. There are 10 values, so the median is the average of the 5th and 6th: $\frac{21+24}{2} = \frac{45}{2} =$ 22.5. We do not actually need this value to find the upper and lower quartiles. We look at the set of numbers below the median: 13, 16, 16, 18, 21. There are five values, so the 3rd is the median (16), or the value of the lower quartile (Q_1). Then we look at the numbers above the median: 24, 27, 32, 39, 51. Again there are five values, so the 3rd is the median (32), or the value of the upper quartile (Q_3). We find the IQR by subtracting Q_1 from Q_3: $32 - 16 = 16$.

68-95-99.7 RULE

The **68–95–99.7 rule** describes how a normal distribution of data should appear when compared to the mean. This is also a description of a normal bell curve. According to this rule, 68 percent of the data values in a normally distributed set should fall within one standard deviation of the mean (34 percent above and 34 percent below the mean), 95 percent of the data values should fall within two standard deviations of the mean (47.5 percent above and 47.5 percent below the mean), and 99.7 percent of the data values should fall within three standard deviations of the mean, again, equally distributed on either side of the mean. This means that only 0.3 percent of all data values should fall more than three standard deviations from the mean. On the graph below, the normal curve is

Inductive Reasoning

centered on the *y*-axis. The *x*-axis labels are how many standard deviations away from the center you are. Therefore, it is easy to see how the 68-95-99.7 rule can apply.

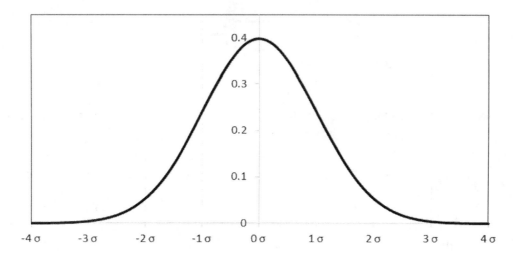

Frequency Distributions

A **frequency distribution** sorts data to give a clear visual representation of the distribution. Numbers are grouped with like numbers (for instance, all numbers in their twenties may be grouped together) to measure the frequency.

EXAMPLE

We can sort the following set of numbers into a frequency distribution based on the value of the tens place: 20, 12, 37, 18, 21, 19, 32, 21, 16, and 14. To do this, we group them into sets by first digit and create a table. This can include just category and frequency, but can also include relative frequency or percentage:

Category	Frequency	Relative Frequency	Percentage
Tens	5	0.5	50%
Twenties	3	0.3	30%
Thirties	2	0.2	20%

We can see that there is a higher concentration of numbers in the tens than any other group. This means that the data will likely be skewed right, with the mean greater than the median.

CUMULATIVE FREQUENCY DISTRIBUTIONS

A **cumulative frequency distribution**, rather than showing the amount in each category, shows the *cumulative* amount. In other words, the amount for each new category is added to each of the previous amounts to show the cumulative sum. This is helpful when the goal is to compare not single groups against each other, but to look at several groups as a sample. For instance, in a cumulative frequency distribution based on employees' salaries, a person could immediately see how many employees make at or below a certain amount per year.

EXAMPLE

A teacher could create a cumulative frequency distribution out of the following test grades: 89, 76, 74, 92, 83, 86, 90, 87, 85, 82, 95, 68, 97, 94, 86, 82, 89, 81, 78, 82. The grades could be divided into groups and placed in a table, adding on each new group to the previous to find the cumulative frequency:

Limits	Frequency	Cumulative frequency
0–75	2	2
76–80	2	4
81–85	6	10
86–90	6	16
91–95	3	19
96–100	1	20

Now the teacher can easily see, for instance, that 10 of the 20 students are scoring at 85 or below.

Scatter Plots

BIVARIATE DATA

Bivariate data is simply data from two different variables. (The prefix *bi-* means *two.*) In a *scatter plot*, each value in the set of data is plotted on a grid similar to a Cartesian plane, where each axis represents one of the two variables. By looking at the pattern formed by the points on the grid, you can often determine whether or not there is a relationship between the two variables, and what that relationship is, if it exists. The variables may be directly proportionate, inversely proportionate, or show no proportion at all. It may also be possible to determine if the data is linear, and if so, to find an equation to relate the two variables. The following scatter plot shows the relationship between preference for brand "A" and the age of the consumers surveyed.

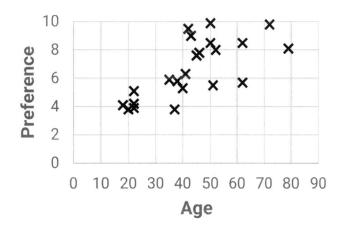

SCATTER PLOTS

Scatter plots are also useful in determining the type of function represented by the data and finding the simple regression. Linear scatter plots may be positive or negative.

Nonlinear scatter plots are generally exponential or quadratic. Below are some common types of scatter plots:

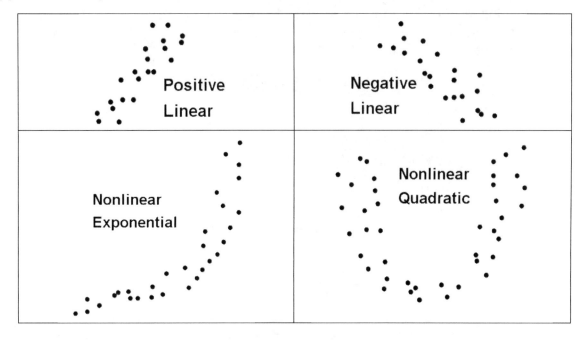

Proportions and Ratios

PROPORTIONS

A proportion is a relationship between two quantities that dictates how one changes when the other changes. A **direct proportion** describes a relationship in which a quantity increases by a set amount for every increase in the other quantity, or decreases by that same amount for every decrease in the other quantity. Example: Assuming a constant driving speed, the time required for a car trip increases as the distance of the trip increases. The distance to be traveled and the time required to travel are directly proportional.

An **inverse proportion** is a relationship in which an increase in one quantity is accompanied by a decrease in the other, or vice versa. Example: the time required for a car trip decreases as the speed increases and increases as the speed decreases, so the time required is inversely proportional to the speed of the car.

RATIOS

A **ratio** is a comparison of two quantities in a particular order. Example: If there are 14 computers in a lab, and the class has 20 students, there is a student to computer ratio of 20

to 14, commonly written as 20: 14. Ratios are normally reduced to their smallest whole number representation, so 20: 14 would be reduced to 10: 7 by dividing both sides by 2.

CONSTANT OF PROPORTIONALITY

When two quantities have a proportional relationship, there exists a **constant of proportionality** between the quantities. The product of this constant and one of the quantities is equal to the other quantity. For example, if one lemon costs $0.25, two lemons cost $0.50, and three lemons cost $0.75, there is a proportional relationship between the total cost of lemons and the number of lemons purchased. The constant of proportionality is the **unit price**, namely $0.25/lemon. Notice that the total price of lemons, t, can be found by multiplying the unit price of lemons, p, and the number of lemons, n: $t = pn$.

WORK/UNIT RATE

Unit rate expresses a quantity of one thing in terms of one unit of another. For example, if you travel 30 miles every two hours, a unit rate expresses this comparison in terms of one hour: in one hour you travel 15 miles, so your unit rate is 15 miles per hour. Other examples are how much one ounce of food costs (price per ounce) or figuring out how much one egg costs out of the dozen (price per 1 egg, instead of price per 12 eggs). The denominator of a unit rate is always 1. Unit rates are used to compare different situations to solve problems. For example, to make sure you get the best deal when deciding which kind of soda to buy, you can find the unit rate of each. If soda #1 costs $1.50 for a 1-liter bottle, and soda #2 costs $2.75 for a 2-liter bottle, it would be a better deal to buy soda #2, because its unit rate is only $1.375 per 1-liter, which is cheaper than soda #1. Unit rates can also help determine the length of time a given event will take. For example, if you can paint 2 rooms in 4.5 hours, you can determine how long it will take you to paint 5 rooms by solving for the unit rate per room and then multiplying that by 5.

Inductive Reasoning

Practice Questions

1. Here are two pie charts about the most recent class to graduate from a city police academy, breaking them down by sex and educational level.

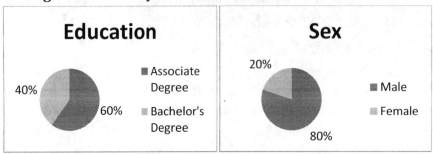

There were one hundred graduates. Half of the female graduates possess a bachelor's degree. How many of the male graduates have a bachelor's degree?

A. 20
B. 25
C. 30
D. 35

2. This table shows the number of times corrections officers called off sick for a shift at four different facilities. The middle column is the number of call-offs in September. The right column represents the number of call-offs in October, when the flu was going around. Assuming that the number of call-offs in September is fairly typical for a normal month, which facility's corrections staff appears to have been least affected by the flu virus?

Facility	September call-offs	October call-offs
Milton	9	12
Ferguson	12	18
Dalton	17	15
Howard	2	6

A. Milton
B. Ferguson
C. Dalton
D. Howard

3. An increasing number of cities are drafting new regulations concerning tattoos on police officers. Up until a couple of decades ago, very few people had tattoos. Among people that were tattooed, most only had one and it was small and covered by clothing. On top of that, the vast majority of people who had a tattoo weren't interested in becoming police officers. Until recently, therefore, many cities had no official policy concerning tattoos on police officers because it was a situation that rarely came up. These days, however, tattoos are much more common, and many people have several, and it's not unusual for these tattoos to be visible even when the person is fully clothed. Here is a table with the number of officers in one county sheriff's department who have 1, 2, 3, or 4+ tattoos, by age range:

Age	1 Tattoo	2 Tattoos	3 Tattoos	4+ Tattoos
22 to 30	15	10	5	1
31 to 45	10	7	5	3
46 to 54	5	5	2	0
55+	3	1	0	0

How many people in the department have at least two tattoos?

    A. 33

    B. 35

    C. 37

    D. 39

Inductive Reasoning

4. Some small towns and villages located near interstate freeways take advantage of that fact by creating speed traps. That is, they set a lower speed limit on the part of the freeway that falls in their jurisdiction. The speed limit changes without warning and for no apparent reason. Many unsuspecting motorists never see the sign about the lower speed limit, or they see it too late, and are essentially tricked into exceeding the artificially low speed limit. The motorists are then pulled over and issued a speeding ticket. For some of these towns, speeding tickets bring in the majority of the local government's revenue. Some state governments are cracking down on this practice, by limiting the percentage of a town's budget that can come from speeding tickets to no more than 30%, and requiring the towns to turn over any amount exceeding that to the state. Here is a chart showing the percentage of municipal revenue brought in by speeding tickets in one state's worst speed traps, before and after the state passed the law capping speeding ticket revenues.

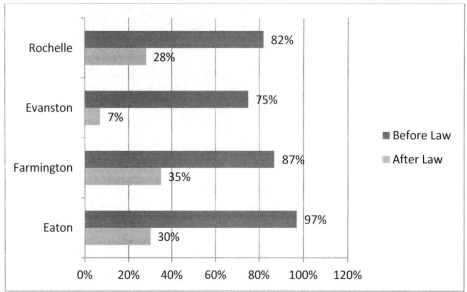

As a percentage, which town had the biggest drop in their revenue from speeding tickets?

  A. Rochelle
  B. Evanston
  C. Farmington
  D. Eaton

5. Here is a table showing the number and kinds of contraband items confiscated last week at four facilities.

Facility	Drugs	Phone	Weapon	Tobacco
Lancaster	3	8	7	12
Charleston	9	1	0	9
Hartwig	12	6	9	2
Wharton	7	9	8	7

Which facility had the most contraband items confiscated last week?

    A. Lancaster
    B. Charleston
    C. Hartwig
    D. Wharton

Inductive Reasoning

Practice Answers

1. C: 40% of 100 is 40, so a total of 40 graduates hold a bachelor's degree. 20% of the graduates are women, and half of them have a bachelors. Half of 20 is 10. If 40 of the graduates have a bachelor's degree, and women have 10, then 30 men have a bachelor's degree.

2. C: Of the four facilities, three had more call-offs in October than in September, but Dalton had fewer. It stands to reason that they weren't as affected by the flu virus.

3. D: To find the correct answer, simply add up all the numbers in the 2, 3, and 4 Tattoo columns, and the total is the correct answer, 39.

4. B: You can do the math using the same formula used in Questions 9 and 13, but that shouldn't be necessary. It should be pretty clear with just a glance that the city of Evanston experienced a far bigger percentage drop in revenue than the other three towns.

5. D: To answer this question, simply add up the number of items in all four categories, for each city, and that's the total number of contraband items confiscated last week. Lancaster had 30, Charleston had 19, Hartwig had 29, and Wharton had 31.

Practice Test

Want to take this practice test in an online interactive format? Check out the bonus page, which includes interactive practice questions and much more: **mometrix.com/bonus948/cjbat**

SCAN HERE

Written Comprehension

1. Beginning at 10:57 on the night of July 23rd, the 911 service received several phone calls reporting a large fight at a night club downtown. Four squad cars with eight officers responded immediately and found about a dozen adult males engaged in a melee. Within five minutes of arriving on the scene, they had the situation under control, and they began interviewing the combatants and witnesses. One of the combatants, Jose Mendez, told Officer Ronald Jones that the fight had begun when another man had assaulted his (Mendez's) date by tossing his drink in her face, and he had responded by punching the man. Officer Shantel Williams interviewed the man Mendez accused of starting the fight, Roland Hemphill, who denied tossing his drink on anyone, and said that he had tripped and accidentally spilled his drink on a woman, whose date then punched him. At this point, according to Hemphill and other witnesses, friends of both parties jumped in to defend their friends. Officer Mark Jones interviewed Tyreese Smith, the bartender, who said that he hadn't seen how it started as he had his back turned toward the crowd at the moment the fight erupted. Several other witnesses, who spoke to Officers Mike Smith and Wendell Brown, backed up Hemphill's account that the drink was spilled accidentally. There were no witnesses who claimed he tossed the drink deliberately. After interviewing nearly everyone on the scene, officers arrested Jose Mendez for battery.

Which officer interviewed the victim of Mendez's battery?
   a. Officer Shantel Williams
   b. Officer Ronald Jones
   c. Officer Mike Smith
   d. Officer Mark Jones

2. At approximately 2:44 p.m., Officer Rafael Sandoz located a stolen motor vehicle in a driveway of a residence in the 2000 block of Fair Havens Drive. The vehicle was unoccupied and it was quickly determined that it had recently been stolen from Orlando. Officer Sandoz called for backup. Shortly thereafter, Officers Macy Blevins and Officer Nick Glenn knocked on the door of the residence, and after identifying themselves and entering the house, questioned several individuals inside with regards to the stolen car. One of the individuals was in possession of suspected illegal narcotics and provided officers with false personal identifying information. She was eventually identified as Asia Campos and she was arrested on an outstanding warrant. While at the same location the three officers discovered another motor vehicle that had been reported stolen from Pensacola parked in

the garage. They also discovered a motorcycle reported stolen from Pensacola behind the house. There were also illegal narcotics inside of the residence. The investigation led to the arrest of Ronald Holderman for the Orlando stolen motorcycle.

How many people were arrested?
   a. One
   b. Two
   c. Three
   d. Four

3. Just prior to Lights Out at a medium-security state prison, corrections staff staged an unannounced search for contraband after receiving several reports that at least two inmates possessed homemade knives and were planning to use them to "settle some scores." Although a thorough search turned up no knives, several contraband items were discovered and seized. Correctional Officer Steve Wilson found a marijuana cigarette in Inmate Reggie Wilson's pillow, and a cup of homemade wine in Inmate Robert Doolittle's cell. Correctional Officer Bob Jackson found a mobile phone in the cell of Inmates Mustafa Johnson and Dewayne Smith; both men denied that the phone was theirs. In a cell shared by Inmates Ryan McDonald and Brent Travers, Correctional Officer Emilio Padilla discovered three syringes and a metal spoon; both inmates claimed that the drug paraphernalia wasn't theirs and they were being "set up."

Altogether, how many contraband items were discovered?
   a. Five
   b. Six
   c. Seven
   d. Eight

4. On June 29 at approximately 11:30 a.m., two officers with from the police department's Southern Division were dispatched to a hotel in the 4500 block of Nevada Ave. to follow up on a missing person report about an adult, later identified as Eleanor Snowden, a 68-year-old female. The investigation revealed that Ms. Snowden registered as a guest of the hotel on June 20 but she has not been seen since June 22. Ms. Snowden has a condition that qualifies her as an at-risk member of the community and as such, our department is asking for assistance in locating her. Ms. Snowden is described as a white female, 5'08", 145 pounds, gray hair with blue eyes, and who was last seen wearing a gray hooded sweatshirt and blue pajama pants. A photograph of Ms. Snowden is available if requested.

How long has Ms. Snowden been missing?
   a. Two days
   b. Five days
   c. Seven days
   d. Ten days

5. Three officers responded to a call about a bank robbery in progress. When they got to the bank, the robbery was over and the criminals were gone. The head teller, Robin Benedict, told Officer Steve Atkins that four men in hoodies had pulled guns, ordered all customers to the floor, and demanded money. The bank's branch manager, Sheila Smith, told Officer Brenda Wilson that the robbers had been given four bags of cash, totaling a little over $20,000, and that tellers managed to get dye packs into three of the four bags. She estimated that one of the robbers was about 6 feet tall and about 180 pounds, one was 6 feet 3 inches and 225 pounds, another was probably around 5 feet 8 inches and 150 pounds, and the other was also about 5 feet 8 inches but weighed around 180 pounds. Each of them fled in a separate getaway vehicle—the tallest one took off going east in a brown van, the second tallest went west on a motorcycle, the short, stocky one fled west in a white Honda Civic, and the other shorter robber drove west in a small pickup truck. Each of the robbers took one bag of cash, but the branch manager wasn't sure which one had the bag without a dye pack.

What was the approximate height and weight of the robber who fled in a pickup truck?

    a. 6 feet 0 inches and 180 lbs
    b. 6 feet 3 inches and 225 lbs
    c. 5 feet 8 inches and 150 lbs
    d. 5 feet 8 inches and 180 lbs

6. During the early morning hours of January 22, patrol officers were dispatched to a residence on South Phelan Boulevard in reference to a felony menacing/shots fired call for service. During the questioning after they arrived on the scene, the officers were told by several witnesses that during a house party for a pay-for-view event, one of the guests, Donte Broomfield, 34 years of age, pulled a handgun. Witnesses stated that Mr. Broomfield threatened four women with the gun and physically assaulted two of them after they all rebuffed his advances. Witnesses further told the officers that Broomfield then left the party with his brother, and fired several rounds at the house as he was driven away by his brother. None of the rounds struck the house, but some of them did strike the vacant house next door. No one was injured during the shooting. Upon further investigation, officers discovered that Broomfield had allegedly pistol-whipped yet another acquaintance with a handgun at a different residence prior to the party. Officers attempted to locate the suspect through the night, but did not find him. It is believed he has fled the area.

How many people did Donte Broomfield assault at the pay-per-view party?

    a. One
    b. Two
    c. Three
    d. Four

7. The corrections supervisor handed out the schedule for the upcoming month. Corrections Officer Jones was assigned to Unit A for the first and third weeks, and Unit D for the second and fourth weeks. Corrections Officer Crews was assigned to Unit B for the first and third weeks, and Unit C for the second and fourth weeks. Corrections Officer Cantrell was assigned to Unit D for the first and third weeks, and Unit A for the second and fourth weeks. Corrections Officer Evers was assigned to Unit C for the first and third weeks, and Unit B for the second and fourth weeks. Corrections Officer Mason was assigned to Unit B for the first and third weeks, and Unit C for the second and fourth weeks. Corrections Officer Espinosa was assigned to Unit A for the first and third weeks, and Unit D for the second and fourth weeks. Corrections Officer Jefferson was assigned to Unit C for the first and third weeks, and Unit D for the second and fourth weeks. Corrections Officer Byers was assigned to Unit B for the first and third weeks, and Unit A for the second and fourth weeks.

Which corrections officers were assigned to Unit C for the second and fourth weeks of the month?

a. Cantrell and Jones
b. Crews and Mason
c. Byers and Cantrell
d. Evers and Jefferson

8. Officers Hollenbeck and Gerson were dispatched to a large department store to answer a call about shoplifting suspects in custody. When they arrived at the store, the customer service clerk directed them to the manager's office in the back. In the small office, they encountered the manager, an assistant manager, two security guards, and four suspects who were being detained. The four suspects identified themselves as Steve Nesmith, Brandon Jackson, Chad Pierson, and Ray Wellstone. All four were white males, and all were 18-19 years of age. A security guard told the officers that they had videotapes of all four suspects taking items and attempting to leave the store without paying. The manager then played the videotapes, which showed Nesmith putting on a hooded sweatshirt and removing the price tag, while Wellstone stuffed a dress down his pants. On another tape, Pierson is seen shoving several bags of candy into his pockets, and on the final tape, Jackson is seen filling his pockets with women's cosmetics. The four suspects admitted that they had taken the items, but told Officers Hollenbeck and Gerson that they were all students at a local university, and their actions were part of a hazing ritual, as they were all attempting to join a fraternity, which had ordered them to steal these items as a "prank." They insisted that they had planned to return and pay for the items after the hazing was over, and asked for leniency because none of them had any prior arrests. The officers arrested all four for shoplifting and then had them transported downtown for processing.

Who stole an item of women's clothing?

a. Nesmith
b. Jackson
c. Pierson
d. Wellstone

9. Officers Regina Petty and Thomas Fritz responded to a call about a loud party in progress at 5792 Windmere Avenue. Arriving at the house at approximately 1:30 AM, they heard loud rap music blaring from the house as soon as they exited their car. A couple dozen people were outside the house, spread out in the yard, on the porch, and on the sidewalk. As they approached the house, a man came out of the house next door and stopped the officers. He said "these people have been nothing but trouble since they moved in a year ago", and it was high time the police cracked down on them. According to the neighbor, within the last six months, police officers had been to the house to investigate public intoxication, another time for a domestic dispute call, a few weeks later for loud music, then again for cars parking illegally and impeding traffic, and the last time for a person who was drunk and disorderly. The officers said they were aware of the recent history of the occupants, and asked the neighbor to go back inside his house. They then approached the party house and asked for the homeowner. When he came to the door, the officers told him to end the party and send everyone home, or everyone there would be charged with disturbing the peace. The homeowner briefly argued with the officers, but then complied with their instructions.

According to the neighbor, how many times had the police been to the house in the last six months?

   a. Five
   b. Six
   c. Seven
   d. Eight

10. Police are searching for a driver who fled from a car after a chase by several officers Tuesday night. At 9:21 p.m., Officer James Logan attempted to stop a vehicle for speeding on Grosvenor Drive. According to Officer Logan, the driver failed to yield and sped off, heading south on Grosvenor, then turning east onto Eldridge Avenue. After nearly causing a collision with another car at the intersection of Scranton Street, he turned north onto Huddleston Pike and appeared to be heading for the freeway. He managed to elude the pursuing officers for only a short time, however, as he lost control of the car when he tried to cut through a parking lot and one of the tires blew out after jumping the curb. The driver fled the scene on foot and has not yet been caught, but he has been identified, according to the report. It was soon discovered that the vehicle had been stolen at approximately 9:15 p.m.

Where did the driver nearly collide with another car?

   a. The onramp of the freeway
   b. Cutting through a parking lot
   c. The intersection of Grosvenor and Eldridge
   d. The intersection of Eldridge and Scranton

11. At approximately 7:00 p.m., Officer John Ramirez and Officer Bettina Woolsey were dispatched to a report of a fight taking place in the 1500 block of Maple Avenue. The caller stated that the males in the house had begun arguing over a football game on TV, which led to a physical altercation, and that one of her sons was unconscious and her nephew was bleeding. When the officers arrived, the woman answered the door and let them in the house, where they found four males who had obviously been fighting. Steven Jones, the woman's husband and the owner of the house, had a torn shirt and a lump on his forehead. His brother, Eric Jones, looked disheveled but didn't have any obvious injuries. Both men appeared to be between 40 and 50 years of age. Mark Jones, the son of Steven Jones and the female caller, and an occupant of the house, was lying on the couch and appeared to be woozy. Ethan Jones, the son of Eric Jones, had a makeshift bandage around his head, which was stained with blood. These two men were in their early twenties. None of the men were very cooperative with the officers. The female who called police said that her son and his cousin were watching a football game when her husband and brother-in-law demanded that they change the station so they could watch a different game. The younger men refused, and that's what started the fight. She said alcohol was also a factor. However, all of the men denied that they needed medical help, and they all refused to press charges, so the officers gave them a stern warning and departed without making any arrests.

Who had a bloody forehead?
   a. Eric Jones
   b. Steven Jones
   c. Mark Jones
   d. Ethan Jones

12. After a series of mass brawls in the TV room of the main unit, prison officials decided to crack down on known or suspected members of prison gangs, by moving them to another unit, or transferring them to another prison. Six members of the Latin Kings were moved to other units, while three were transferred. Four members of the Outlaws were moved to other units, while two were transferred. Four members of the Gangster Disciples were moved to other units, while six were transferred. Seven members of the Mexican Mafia were moved to other units, while two were transferred. After these changes, violence in the main unit decreased substantially, while violence in the other units did not increase.

Which prison gang saw the most members moved out of the unit or transferred?
   a. Mexican Mafia
   b. Outlaws
   c. Gangster Disciples
   d. Latin Kings

13. At approximately 9:30 p.m. on Wednesday, several officers were dispatched to the Bent Tree Gardens apartment complex at the intersection of Bent Tree Road and 14th Avenue, in response to calls about a large group of people fighting. Callers said the group had been arguing and screaming at each other for nearly two hours, and were on the verge of brawling. Upon arrival from a side alley, officers counted ten men and eight women in the brightly lit parking lot, divided into two groups facing each other, and heard many of them exchanging threats of violence. When the crowd realized police had arrived, they took off running in various directions. All escaped except for two women, who were arrested and transported downtown for processing. Shortly after midnight, 911 callers reported that the group was back in the parking lot, again disturbing the peace and threatening to fight. This time, a larger number of officers responded, and while many of the brawlers successfully fled on foot, officers were able to detain five men and three women. One of the men and two of the women were determined to be bystanders, and let go, but the rest were arrested and taken in for booking.

How many women were arrested?

    a. One
    b. Two
    c. Three
    d. Four

14. On Tuesday, 09/22, at approximately 4:11 a.m., a call for service was received about a rollover car accident in the area of Greenhills Blvd. and Robertson Rd. When they arrived on the scene, officers located a single vehicle on the sidewalk on the south side of the eastbound lanes of Greenhills Blvd., just west of Robertson Rd. That vehicle, a Toyota Corolla, had left the roadway and rolled over, landing on its roof, ejecting two female occupants and trapping two additional male occupants. All occupants were transported by ambulance to area hospitals. The driver, who was identified as 26-year-old Caitlyn Malcolm, was evaluated and arrested for DUI and Vehicular Assault. The 22-year-old female passenger, Britney Maddox, is currently being treated for serious injuries. The 26-year-old and 29-year-old male passengers, Ryan Tellinger and Rob Tellinger, were treated for less serious injuries and discharged from the hospital. The eastbound lanes of Greenhills Blvd. were temporarily closed to facilitate the investigation. The Major Accidents Unit responded to conduct the investigation in conjunction with the originally responding patrol officers.

Who was charged with Vehicular Assault?

    a. Britney Maddox
    b. Caitlyn Malcolm
    c. Rob Tellinger
    d. Ryan Tellinger

15. After a recent surge of violent crimes in a local neighborhood, gang activity suppression officers were out in force last weekend, and made several arrests. On Friday night, they made three arrests for selling drugs, five for loitering, six for public intoxication, and nine for outstanding warrants. On Saturday afternoon, they made two arrests for selling drugs, nine for loitering, and five for outstanding warrants. On Saturday night and into early Sunday morning, they arrested fifteen people for outstanding warrants, seven for selling drugs, ten for loitering, and six for public intoxication. Police officials said the crackdown will continue until the neighborhood sees a significant reduction in the crime rate.

Altogether, how many people were arrested for selling drugs during the crackdown?

a. Three
b. Six
c. Nine
d. Twelve

Written Expression

1. The depudy talked to the sheriff about possibly going back to school and earning a bachelor's degree.

One word in the above sentence is misspelled. It is:
   a. depudy
   b. sheriff
   c. possibly
   d. bachelor's

2. The witness _____ the suspect as a man in his late twenties.

Which of these words would be the correct choice to fill in the blank?
   a. subscribed
   b. prescribed
   c. described
   d. ascribed

3. The prison transport van arived over two hours late, requiring the officers to have to fill out overtime authorization forms.

One word in the above sentence is misspelled. It is:
   a. transport
   b. arived
   c. requiring
   d. authorization

4. If you will have to miss work due to illness, you _____ notify the department no later than two hours before your shift starts.

Which of these words or phrases would be the correct choice to fill in the blank?
   a. are
   b. have
   c. must
   d. must have

5. The robbery took place in broad daylight, shocking many of the small town's cittizens.

One word in the above sentence is misspelled. It is:
   a. robbery
   b. broad
   c. shocking
   d. cittizens

6. NOTICE: It _____ not permitted to carry a concealed weapon on these premises.

Which of these words would be the correct choice to fill in the blank?
a. is
b. am
c. isn't
d. are

7. The funural procession for the mayor consisted of over one hundred vehicles.

One word in the above sentence is misspelled. It is:
a. funural
b. procession
c. consisted
d. vehicles

8. At roll call, everyone will be _____ his or her rounds for the day.

Which of these words or phrases would be the correct choice to fill in the blank?
a. have assigned
b. assigned
c. requested
d. required

9. The weather report brought unpleasent news—there's a possibility of a tornado.

One word in the above sentence is misspelled. It is:
a. weather
b. unpleasent
c. possibility
d. tornado

10. The best policy is to always _____ prepared for the worst.

Which of these words or phrases would be the correct choice to fill in the blank?
a. been
b. to be
c. are being
d. be

11. The sergeant will summarize his findings for the cheif, who will prepare a report for the mayor.

One word in the above sentence is misspelled. It is:

    a. sergeant
    b. summarize
    c. cheif
    d. mayor

12. No one will _____ the academy without first passing a background check.

Which of these words or phrases would be the correct choice to fill in the blank?

    a. allowed to
    b. admitted to
    c. be allowed to
    d. be admitted to

13. The outgoing union president said the membership would pay a steap price for voting him out.

One word in the above sentence is misspelled. It is:

    a. outgoing
    b. membership
    c. steap
    d. voting

14. The police spokesman said extra patrols _____ added downtown due to the number of robberies going up 25% in six months.

Which of these words or phrases would be the correct choice to fill in the blank?

    a. have been
    b. has been
    c. have
    d. been

15. The corrections officer orientation manual states clearly that officers are not allowed to endorse any politician or attend any political functions while in uniform.

One word in the above sentence is misspelled. It is:

    a. orientation
    b. manual
    c. endorce
    d. functions

This page is intentionally left blank.

Memorization

This section contains several photographs. Study each picture for one minute. Then turn the page and answer some questions about the picture.

Photo 1

1. How many people appear in this photo?

    a. 12

    b. 13

    c. 14

    d. 15

2. How many people in the first row are wearing a dress?

    a. 0

    b. 1

    c. 2

    d. 3

Photo 2

3. Of the three people in the main area of the picture, how many are wearing glasses?

    a. 0
    b. 1
    c. 2
    d. 3

4. What is the woman whose luggage the dog is sniffing doing?

    a. Taking a nap
    b. Looking at her phone
    c. Talking to a police officer
    d. Reading a book

Photo 3

5. Which officer is taller?

   a.   Both officers are the same height
   b.   It's impossible to tell from the picture
   c.   The officer on the left
   d.   The officer on the right.

6. Which officer is wearing sunglasses?

   a.   Neither one
   b.   Both
   c.   The officer on the left
   d.   The officer on the right

7. Which officer is in short sleeves?

   a.   Neither one
   b.   Both
   c.   The officer on the left
   d.   The officer on the right

8. Which officer is wearing a cap?

   a.   Neither one
   b.   Both
   c.   The officer on the left
   d.   The officer on the right

9. Which officer is wearing gloves?

   a.   Neither one
   b.   Both
   c.   The officer on the left
   d.   The officer on the right

Photo 4

Practice Test

10. Which officer is tallest?

   a.   The officer on the left
   b.   The officer in the middle
   c.   The officer on the right
   d.   They are all about the same height

11. Which officer is holding his beverage in his right hand?

   a.   The officer on the left
   b.   The officer in the middle
   c.   The officer on the right
   d.   All of them

12. What does the street sign say?

   a.   42nd St
   b.   42nd Ave
   c.   24th St
   d.   24th Ave

Photo 5

13. According to the mileage sign, how far away is Condon?

    a. 38 miles

    b. 138 miles

    c. 159 miles

    d. 59 miles

14. Which sign is taller?

    a. The mileage sign

    b. The road sign

    c. Both signs are the same height

    d. It's impossible to tell from the picture

15. In which direction is the arrow on the road sign pointing?

    a. Right

    b. Left

    c. Up

    d. Down

Deductive Reasoning

1. Money Laundering

(a) A person commits an offense if the person knowingly:

(1) acquires or maintains an interest in, conceals, possesses, transfers, or transports the proceeds of criminal activity;

(2) conducts, supervises, or facilitates a transaction involving the proceeds of criminal activity;

(3) invests, expends, or receives, or offers to invest, expend, or receive, the proceeds of criminal activity or funds that the person believes are the proceeds of criminal activity; or

(4) finances or invests or intends to finance or invest funds that the person believes are intended to further the commission of criminal activity.

(a-1) Knowledge of the specific nature of the criminal activity giving rise to the proceeds is not required to establish a culpable mental state under this section.

(b) It is a defense to prosecution under this section that the person acted with intent to facilitate the lawful seizure, forfeiture, or disposition of funds or other legitimate law enforcement purpose pursuant to the laws of this state or the US

(c) It is a defense to prosecution under this section that the transaction was necessary to preserve a person's right to representation as guaranteed by the Sixth Amendment of the United States Constitution and by Article 1, Section 10, of the Texas Constitution or that the funds were received as bona fide legal fees by a licensed attorney and at the time of their receipt, the attorney did not have actual knowledge that the funds were derived from criminal activity.

(d) An offense under this section is:

(1) a state jail felony if the value of the funds is $2,500 or more but less than $30,000;

(2) a felony of the third degree if the value of the funds is $30,000 or more but less than $150,000;

(3) a felony of the second degree if the value of the funds is $150,000 or more but less than $300,000; or

(4) a felony of the first degree if the value of the funds is $300,000 or more.

A woman suspects her husband has started selling drugs out of their rural home while she works during the day. When she finds $38,000 in cash hidden in a closet, she is convinced of it. Wanting no part of the illicit operation, and fearing arrest, one day while her husband is away, she puts the cash in the trunk of her car and begins driving to the county sheriff's office nearly ten miles away. On her way there, a state trooper pulls her over for speeding, and when he discovers the cash, arrests her for suspicious activity. Based on the information above, what level of felony will the woman most likely be charged with?

    a. First degree felony
    b. Second degree felony
    c. Third degree felony
    d. She will face no charges

2. Here are some rules from the Police Officer Manual for a large city. Breaking any of these rules can result in receiving disciplinary action, up to and including being fired:

Rule 25: Failure to inventory and process recovered property in conformance with department orders.

Rule 27: Disseminating, releasing, altering, defacing or removing any department record or information concerning police matters except as provided by department orders.

Rule 28: Participating in any partisan political campaign or activity.

Rule 29: Associating or fraternizing with any person known to have been convicted of any felony or misdemeanor, either State or Federal, excluding traffic and municipal ordinance violations.

Rule 30: Discussing bail with a person who is in custody except by those specifically authorized to let to bond.

Rule 32: Giving an opinion as to fine or penalty.

Rule 34: Recommending any professional or commercial service.

Rule 37: Advising any person engaged in a professional or commercial service that such professional or commercial services may be needed.

Rule 41: Soliciting or accepting any gratuity, or soliciting or accepting a gift, present, reward, or other thing of value for any service rendered as a department member, or as a condition for the rendering of such service, or as a condition for not performing sworn duties.

You are a police officer who has sworn to follow the above rules. You're also a member of a neighborhood softball team, which you have played on for several years. At the first meeting for the upcoming season, you learn that a new member of the team is a convicted felon. He was released from prison five years ago after being sentenced for grand theft auto. However, he has not been in any trouble with the law in the five years since his parole, has a respectable job, and has started a family. Based on the above information, what should you do?

    a. Nothing, as the man is no longer a criminal
    b. Associate with him at games, but not anywhere else
    c. Quit the team immediately
    d. Talk the situation over with your immediate supervisor

3. From the Florida Administrative Code:

(1) When any employee or person supervising inmates witnesses an act or has reason to believe that an act has been committed by an inmate which is in violation of the rules or procedures of the Department and that employee determines that the infraction can be properly disposed of without a formal disciplinary report, the employee shall take the necessary action to resolve the matter.

(2) If the employee cannot resolve the matter through a verbal reprimand or corrective consultation, the employee shall consult with and obtain approval from his or her supervisor regarding preparation of a formal disciplinary report, unless the employee is at the department head level or correctional officer lieutenant level or above.

(3) When it appears that laws of the state have been violated, the Office of the Inspector General shall be notified, who will, in turn, contact the State Attorney when deemed appropriate. If the State Attorney decides to prosecute, his office shall be consulted as to the suitability of disciplinary action being taken by the institution prior to the prosecution being concluded.

(4) The commission of acts that should normally result in consideration for formal disciplinary action shall not be subject to such action when these acts are directly associated with an inmate's intentional self-injurious behavior.

According to the above information, which of these situations would not result in an inmate being punished?

    a. An inmate smoking a cigarette in a no-smoking area
    b. An inmate burning his arm with a lit cigarette
    c. An inmate smoking marijuana
    d. An inmate possessing a cell phone

4. From the Florida Administrative Code:

(1) The following grooming standards shall apply to all Department of Corrections employees, including all non-uniformed employees and contracted employees, while performing official duties:

(a) All employees shall maintain a professional appearance at all times while performing official duties.

(b) All employees shall maintain personal hygiene and shall keep themselves personally neat and clean while on duty.

(c) Clothing will be clean and pressed as is appropriate for the particular garment.

(d) Clothing shall be appropriate for the particular assignment.

(e) Shoes will be clean, presentable, and appropriate for the particular assignment.

(f) Policies regarding the wearing of neck ties for office staff will be determined by the Secretary, Deputy Secretary and Office Directors.

(g) Hair will be neat, clean, trimmed and present a groomed appearance. If the hair is dyed, only natural shades will be permitted.

(h) Earrings are prohibited for male staff. Earrings for female staff will constitute the only body piercing ornaments allowed. No employee will display while on duty any other jewelry of which any part has been pierced into or through the skin or flesh of any part of the body.

(i) Undergarments shall not be visible.

(j) All employees shall dress in a manner appropriate to their positions and duties and shall avoid eccentricities in their personal appearance.

(k) All employees shall dress in a manner required by the court for all court appearances.

A female corrections officer shows up for work one day wearing earrings and with blue frosted highlights in her hair. Which of the above would she be violating?

    a. (f)
    b. (g)
    c. (h)
    d. (j)

5. From the Florida Administrative Code:

(1) Only five approved visitors, 12 years of age or older, at any time, may visit an inmate in the visiting area. Children 11 years old and younger do not count against the five approved visitors.

(2) A visitor's initial check-in shall take place in a location that minimizes weather exposure and provides restrooms.

(3) Visitors shall be required to register for visiting through the automated visiting record. The failure to do so or providing false information shall result in denial or termination of the visit and suspension of visiting privileges.

(4) All visitors sixteen years of age or older must present a valid form of picture identification for visiting registration. Acceptable forms of identification are identification cards that contain a photograph, current address, and date of birth and physical characteristics of the individual. Signatures are not required if the identification otherwise complies with all other standards of proper identification.

(5) A visitor seventeen years old or younger who cannot furnish proof of emancipation must be accompanied during a visit by an approved parent, legal guardian, or authorized adult and must remain under the supervision of that adult at all times, to include when the minor is subject to being searched under the provisions of Rule 33-601.726, F.A.C. An authorized non-parental adult accompanying a visiting minor must provide a notarized document of guardianship from the minor's parent or legal guardian (neither of which may be an inmate except as provided below) granting permission for the minor to visit a specifically identified inmate. The document shall be notarized by someone other than the non-parental adult accompanying the minor and shall be updated every six months from the date of issue. In cases where it can be determined that legal custody remains with the incarcerated parent or legal guardian and has not been given to another adult by the court, a notarized statement from the incarcerated parent or guardian shall be acceptable for purposes of authorizing children of the inmate to visit. Any such authorization remains subject to any relevant court orders or relevant departmental rules regarding the inmate's contact with the minor in question. Falsification of a document of guardianship shall result in the person being subject to suspension of visiting privileges pursuant to paragraph 33-601.731(9)(d), F.A.C.

According to the above, which children need to register through the automated visiting record?
  a. All children
  b. Children eleven years of age or older
  c. Children twelve years of age or older
  d. Children sixteen years of age or older

6. Sale or possession of illegal fireworks:

(4)(a) "Fireworks" means and includes any combustible or explosive composition or substance or combination of substances or, except as hereinafter provided, any article prepared for the purpose of producing a visible or audible effect by combustion, explosion, deflagration, or detonation. The term includes blank cartridges and toy cannons in which explosives are used, the type of balloons which require fire underneath to propel them, firecrackers, torpedoes, skyrockets, roman candles, dago bombs, and any fireworks containing any explosives or flammable compound or any tablets or other device containing any explosive substance.

(b) "Fireworks" does not include sparklers approved by the division pursuant to s. 791.013; toy pistols, toy canes, toy guns, or other devices in which paper caps containing twenty-five hundredths grains or less of explosive compound are used, providing they are so constructed that the hand cannot come in contact with the cap when in place for the explosion; and toy pistol paper caps which contain less than twenty hundredths grains of explosive mixture, the sale and use of which shall be permitted at all times.

(c) "Fireworks" also does not include the following novelties and trick noisemakers:

1. A snake or glow worm, which is a pressed pellet of not more than 10 grams of pyrotechnic composition that produces a large, snakelike ash which expands in length as the pellet burns and that does not contain mercuric thiocyanate.

2. A smoke device, which is a tube or sphere containing not more than 10 grams of pyrotechnic composition that, upon burning, produces white or colored smoke as the primary effect.

3. A trick noisemaker, which is a device that produces a small report intended to surprise the user and which includes:

a. A party popper, which is a small plastic or paper device containing not more than 16 milligrams of explosive composition that is friction sensitive, which is ignited by pulling a string protruding from the device, and which expels a paper streamer and produces a small report.
b. A booby trap, which is a small tube with a string protruding from both ends containing not more than 16 milligrams of explosive compound, which is ignited by pulling the ends of the string, and which produces a small report.
c. A snapper, which is a small, paper-wrapped device containing not more than four milligrams of explosive composition coated on small bits of sand, and which, when dropped, explodes, producing a small report. A snapper may not contain more than 250 milligrams of total sand and explosive composition.
d. A trick match, which is a kitchen or book match which is coated with not more than 16 milligrams of explosive or pyrotechnic composition and which, upon ignition, produces a small report or shower of sparks.

Which of the following falls under the definition of illegal fireworks?
   a. Trick match
   b. Party popper
   c. Toy gun
   d. Roman candle

7. Abuse, aggravated abuse, and neglect of a child; penalties.

(a) A person who willfully or by culpable negligence neglects a child and in so doing causes great bodily harm, permanent disability, or permanent disfigurement to the child commits a felony of the second degree.

(b) A person who knowingly or willfully abuses a child without causing great bodily harm, permanent disability, or permanent disfigurement to the child commits a felony of the third degree.

(c) A person who willfully or by culpable negligence neglects a child without causing great bodily harm, permanent disability, or permanent disfigurement to the child commits a felony of the third degree.

You have been dispatched to a house because neighbors called the police saying the woman who lives there lets her six-year-old and eight-year-old children play in the street long after it gets dark. When you arrive at 10:15 pm, the children are indeed playing in the street, but appear to be healthy and have no injuries. You arrest the woman for her actions. According to the above what kind of crime has she committed?
   a. Misdemeanor
   b. Third-degree felony
   c. Second-degree felony
   d. First-degree felony

8. Gang-related offenses; enhanced penalties.

Upon a finding by the factfinder that the defendant committed the charged offense for the purpose of benefiting, promoting, or furthering the interests of a criminal gang, the penalty for any felony or misdemeanor, or any delinquent act or violation of law which would be a felony or misdemeanor if committed by an adult, may be enhanced. Penalty enhancement affects the applicable statutory maximum penalty only. Each of the findings required as a basis for such sentence shall be found beyond a reasonable doubt. The enhancement will be as follows:

(1)(a) A misdemeanor of the second degree may be punished as if it were a misdemeanor of the first degree.

(b) A misdemeanor of the first degree may be punished as if it were a felony of the third degree. For purposes of sentencing under chapter 921 and determining incentive gain-time eligibility under chapter 944, such offense is ranked in level 1 of the offense severity ranking chart. The criminal gang multiplier in s. 921.0024 does not apply to misdemeanors enhanced under this paragraph.

(2)(a) A felony of the third degree may be punished as if it were a felony of the second degree.

(b) A felony of the second degree may be punished as if it were a felony of the first degree.

(c) A felony of the first degree may be punished as if it were a life felony.

Which of the following is true about enhanced penalties for gang-related offenses?
a. A third-degree felony is treated as a misdemeanor
b. A second-degree felony is treated as a third-degree felony
c. A first-degree misdemeanor is treated as a third-degree felony
d. A life felony is treated as a capital offense

9. Handicapped parking spaces:

In the case of a vehicle illegally parked in an official marked handicapped parking space, the responding officer must have the vehicle removed, either by the driver, or by an authorized tow truck. The vehicle can be removed to a municipal lot, a city garage, or a non-handicapped parking space. If the car's driver is nearby, the officer may order the person to move the vehicle. The officer shall cite the driver for parking in a handicapped parking space without the required permit.

At his/her discretion, the officer may order the driver to produce an official handicapped parking permit. If the officer does so, and the driver refuses to produce the permit, the officer may charge the driver with resisting an officer without violence.

Leaving a mall after investigating a shoplifting incident, you notice a car that doesn't have a handicapped parking permit parked in a handicapped parking space. As you leave your patrol car and approach the vehicle, a man comes out of the mall and approaches the car with keys in hand. You ask him for his disabled parking permit. He says he doesn't have one but since he's now leaving, it's no big deal.

Which of the following would NOT be a proper response by you?
a. Have the car towed and cite the man for illegal use of a handicapped space
b. Give the man a warning about parking in handicapped parking spaces without a permit
c. Cite the man for illegal use of a handicapped space
d. Order the man to move the car, cite him for illegal use of a handicapped space and arrest him for resisting an officer without violence

10. Police Vehicles Involved in Auto Accidents
1. The officer driving a police vehicle involved in any vehicular accident will:
   a. Allow all vehicles involved in the accident to remain in the post-accident position if traffic conditions permit. Except in emergencies, vehicles should not be moved from the scene.

b. Render first aid (if needed) and arrange transportation for the injured (if needed).

c. Immediately request Emergency Communication Center to send a district car and district/section/unit supervisor to investigate the accident.

You are patrolling a residential neighborhood. You've just pulled into a four-way intersection, after stopping at a stop sign, when a car comes from your right and collides with the rear passenger side of your patrol car, doing substantial damage. You are shaken up, but don't seem to have any injuries. The other driver is semi-conscious, and appears to be in serious pain, but there are no visible injuries. What should you do first?

a. Call for an ambulance
b. Render first aid
c. Call the ECC and request a district car and supervisor
d. Move the vehicles out of the roadway

Questions 11-13 are based on the following information:

Criminal trespass is defined as entering someone else's property without permission, or remaining on the property after being told to leave.

Burglary is defined as entering a building without the permission of the owner or tenant, for the purpose of committing a crime.

Theft is defined as taking someone else's property without their permission.

Home invasion is defined as forcefully entering an occupied dwelling for the purpose of committing a felony against one or more occupants.

11. A couple invites several friends and co-workers to their house for a football watching party. Unbeknownst to the couple, one of the invited co-workers is an ex-con. He has heard through the grapevine that the couple keeps a lot of valuables in the house, and he accepts their invitation in hopes of stealing something. Sometime during the party, he is caught in the act of pocketing a necklace from the jewelry box in the couple's bedroom. The couple calls the police. What should he be charged with?

a. Criminal trespass
b. Burglary
c. Theft
d. Home invasion

12. A man is out jogging in a residential neighborhood when he experiences severe stomach cramps. Seeing a home that appears to be unoccupied, he tries the front door, and it turns out to be unlocked. He goes in and uses the bathroom. While he's in the bathroom, the person who is renting the house comes home and discovers him there, and calls the police. What should he be charged with?

   a. Criminal trespass
   b. Burglary
   c. Theft
   d. Home invasion

13. Two men, Steve and Wayne, have been making plans to start a remodeling business as partners. However, the two have a serious falling out, and drop their plans to go into business together when Wayne accuses Steve of trying to take advantage of him financially. A few nights later Wayne and a couple of his friends show up at Steve's front door. They demand that Steve pay Wayne back for his "wasted time." Steve says he doesn't owe Wayne anything, and refuses to let them in. He orders them to leave. Instead, they kick the door in, and threaten to come back and beat Steve if he doesn't pay up within a week. Before they leave, they take some power tools from the garage and inform Steve he'll get them back when he pays what he owes. After they leave, Steve calls the police. What should Wayne and his friends be charged with?

   a. Burglary
   b. Home invasion
   c. Criminal trespass and theft
   d. Home invasion and theft

Questions 14 and 15 are based on the following information:

> When dealing with a strike, picket line, or other dispute involving demonstrations or picketing, there is always a potential for things to quickly get out of control if police don't do their job properly. In such situations, a supervisor will meet with leaders or officials from both labor and management. The supervisor will inform both sides that the role of the police is to protect life and property, and that police officers cannot take either side in the dispute, but are there only to maintain public order and keep the peace.

> The supervisor shall also explain to each side their rights, as well as the rights of the opposing side. They will also inform each side of its responsibilities in the situation, including the obligation to obey all laws, and to obey all lawful orders from police officers. Neither the supervisor nor any officer will under any circumstances discuss the dispute itself, or any other

controversial matters, or state any opinion about labor, management, or the dispute.

If arrests are necessary, the following guidelines should be followed:

5. When it comes to shouting, "trash talking", etc., arrests should be kept to a minimum. Strive to prevent these behaviors from escalating, but arrests should be a last resort.
6. For minor disputes such as those above, the best tactic is to separate the offending parties, and order them to leave the area, with a warning that they will face arrest if they return.
7. When possible, arrests should be made immediately for assaults (threats), shoving, punching, or other instances of battery, intentionally damaging property, or inciting to riot.
8. In some situations an immediate arrest could lead to a situation getting out of hand—if it looks as if supporters are going to form a mob if you arrest a person, and there aren't enough officers on hand to deal with the situation, the situation could rapidly become dangerous to the public, yourself, and other officers. In a situation like this, it's best not to make an immediate arrest. Instead, note the perpetrator and make the arrest later when things are more under control.
9. Always stay on top of the situation and if it looks as if you may need more officers, call for them before they're needed. Simply having more officers arrive can often be enough to prevent things from escalating, or quickly bring violence to a halt.
10. If an arrest is necessary, remove the arrested person from the scene in order to prevent sympathizers from using him/her to stir up the crowd to engage in violence.

14. On a hot summer afternoon, you and another officer have been dispatched to a factory where around 100 angry workers have walked off the job and have formed a large and loud gathering near the entrance to the factory. Several managers stand between the crowd and the building and order the workers to come back in at once or risk being fired. Several of the workers approach you and your fellow officer demanding that the managers be arrested for violating their rights by not providing air conditioning. One of them is using extremely offensive language to describe the managers. They ask you if you think it's humane to make employees work in a factory without air conditioning. You should:

a. Arrest the person who is using foul language for disorderly conduct.
b. Agree that it's inhumane, but say that because it's not illegal, there's nothing you can do.
c. Take the managers aside and ask them to provide air conditioning for the workers.
d. Order the person using the foul language to leave the area or face arrest for disorderly conduct

15. In the same situation as Question 14, as you and your partner get out of your patrol car a manager waves you over. You both go over and speak to him. He says that one of the workers has damaged the building by spray painting some graffiti on it, which is clearly visible. He demands that you arrest the worker in question, who still has the paint can in his hand. The worker admits painting the graffiti and dares you to arrest him, and the crowd joins in, saying that if you try to arrest him you'll have to arrest all of them. You should:

    a. Inform the manager that you can't take sides in the dispute so there's nothing you can do.

    b. Make no arrests and call for backup.

    c. Make no arrests and call for backup, and when enough officers are on the scene arrest the worker for the property damage.

    d. Arrest the worker, after telling the crowd that anyone who tries to interfere will also be arrested.

Mⓞmetrix

Practice Test

Inductive Reasoning

1. One city passed a controversial ordinance in 2002, making it the law that if a person who had been named as the victim of a domestic assault refused to testify, they were required to undergo a minimum of three counseling sessions within six months or pay a $1000 fine. The city council said their immediate goal in passing the law was to encourage abuse victims not to give in to intimidation from their abusers, and their long-term goal was to reduce the incidence of domestic violence by sending more abusers to prison for a year or more. In 2010, the law was ruled unconstitutional by the courts, but we can look at several years of data to see if the law achieved its intended goals. Here are two charts that show the percentage of domestic abuse cases in which the victim refused to testify, and the number of cases of domestic abuse in which the abuser was sentenced to prison for a year or more, for several years after the law was passed.

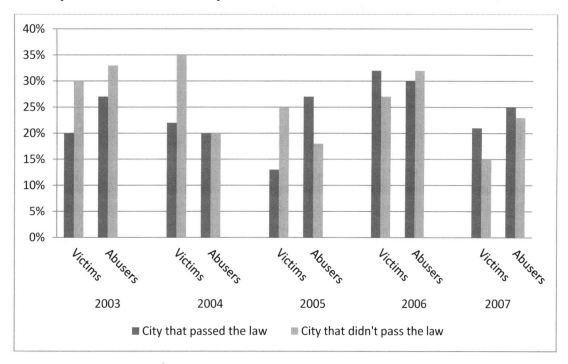

For the city that didn't pass the law, in which two years did the highest percentage of victims agree to testify?

    a. 2005 and 2007

    b. 2003 and 2005

    c. 2005 and 2006

    d. 2003 and 2007

2. After a string of several high-profile car wrecks caused by drunk drivers resulted in the deaths of multiple children during the holiday season one year, the city council decided to focus their efforts on reducing the number of bartenders who are willing to serve customers who've had too much to drink. They passed a law requiring all establishments that serve alcohol to prominently display a poster urging customers to call a hotline and turn in bartenders who continue to serve customers who are clearly drunk. During the first year, exactly one hundred people called the hotline to report a bartender serving a drunken customer. Here is a chart breaking down the calls by month.

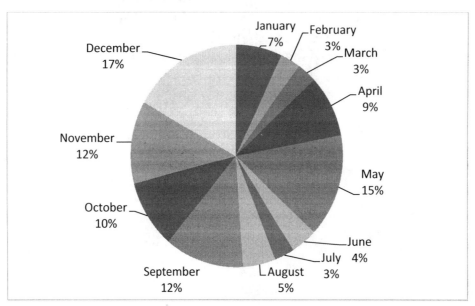

In which month did the greatest number of people call the hotline?

   a. November
   b. September
   c. May
   d. December

3. Here is a chart of major crimes in one American city for the years 2001, 2005, 2009, and 2013.

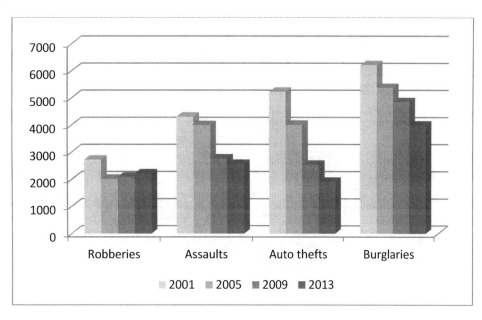

In which year were there fewer auto thefts than robberies?

    a. 2001
    b. 2005
    c. 2009
    d. 2013

4. Here is some data about sex abusers in one city, showing the categories of relationships sexual abusers have with their victims, and what percentage of abusers are in each category, for the years 2011 and 2014.

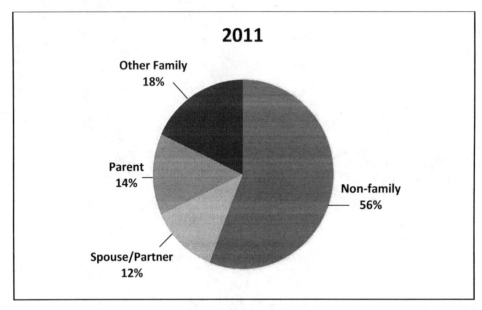

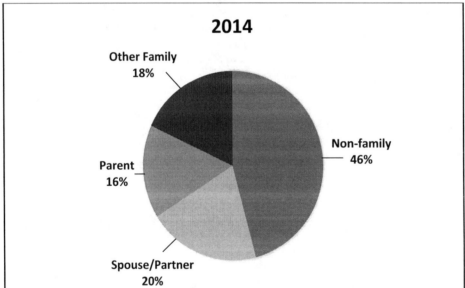

In 2014, which category saw the biggest increase from 2011?

    a. Spouse/Partner
    b. Parent
    c. Other family
    d. Non-family

5. Here are two pie charts showing the geographic origins of all undocumented immigrants arrested for being in the country illegally for the years 2010 and 2011 in one major city.

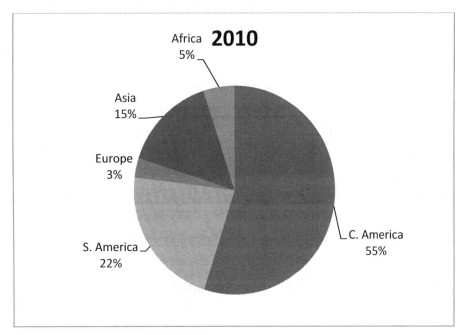

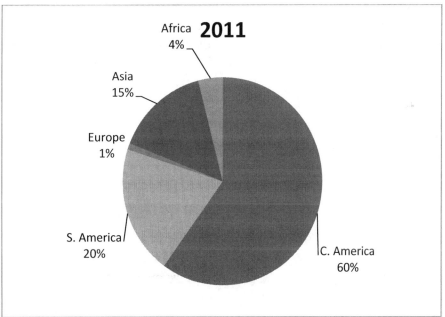

Which geographic area accounted for the same percentage of undocumented workers in both years?

    a. Asia
    b. Europe
    c. South America
    d. Central America

6. There is no longer any argument about whether or not red-light cameras reduce red-light running. The evidence is in, and they clearly do. However, experts say that they should not be installed at an intersection merely because a lot of people run red lights there. Two factors should exist at the intersection before installing a red-light camera—drivers running red lights at a rate at least 25% higher than at the average light, and a percentage of accidents caused by people running red lights that is at least 10% higher than at the average traffic light. There are six intersections being considered for red light cameras.

Intersection	Red-Light Runners	Red-Light Running Accidents
1	1.10	0.95
2	1.25	1.00
3	0.95	1.25
4	1.25	1.15
5	1.10	1.10
6	1.30	1.10

In the table above, Column 2 shows the percentage of drivers who run the red light as a percentage of the average number of drivers who run red lights at all intersections. Column 3 shows the percentage of accidents at that intersection which were caused by people running red lights, compared to the average number of accidents caused by people running red lights at all intersections. Percentages are expressed in decimal form, so 1.0 is average, 1.50 is 50% above average, 0.75 is 25% below average, etc. Using the above standards, which two intersections above should get red light cameras?

    a. 2 and 5
    b. 4 and 6
    c. 1 and 4
    d. 5 and 6

7. The city manager is considering outfitting all patrol cars with new emergency light systems. One company says their design incorporates a newly developed system of colors and patterns that can significantly improve visibility, reducing delays and accidents involving patrol cars. The city manager agreed to install the system on four patrol cars for 30 days, and if at the end of the trial response times for those four cars have been cut by an average of 15 seconds or more, she will authorize the purchase of a system for all patrol cars.

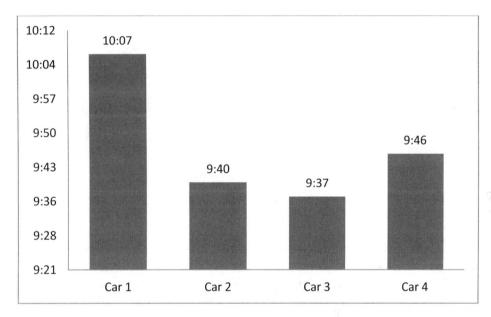

The benchmark, or the average response time before the trial that the test results would be measured against, was 10:00. At the end of the trial, Car 1 had an average response time of 10:06, Car 2 had an average response time of 9:39, Car 3 had an average response time of 9:37, and Car 4 had an average response time of 9:45. Which of the following is true of the average response time of the cars in the trial?

    a. It was lower than the benchmark by 15.5 seconds
    b. It was higher than the benchmark by 15.5 seconds
    c. It was lower than the benchmark by 12.5 seconds
    d. It was higher than the benchmark by 12.5 seconds

8. After learning that its budget wouldn't increase from the previous year due to municipal belt-tightening, the police department in one city was looking for ways to be more effective without spending more money. They decided to park empty patrol cars near stretches of roads which had high accident rates due to speeding. The empty cars would be close enough to be a visible deterrent, but far enough away from the road that it wasn't obvious that the cars were empty. At first, this worked well, and the accident rate declined for a few months. However, drivers eventually realized that the cars were empty, and speed picked up again, as did the accident rate. Then the department began randomly posting officers in cars where the empty cars had been and rotating between manned and unmanned cars on an unpredictable basis. It took a few months, but after drivers began to realize that they could never be sure if the patrol cars were manned or not, they began slowing down again, and the accident rate once again declined.

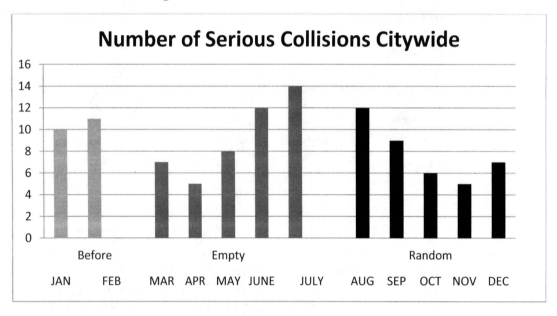

Which of these pairs of months had the same number of accidents?
   a. January and September
   b. February and June
   c. May and November
   d. June and August

9. Preventing people from smuggling contraband to prisoners is one of the most difficult but most important functions a prison administration is charged with, but it's a never-ending battle. In one state, an experiment was tried in hopes of reducing contraband smuggling—at half the prisons, a change was made to the sign which is posted at the visitor's entrance to every facility. The sign, which is 12 inches tall and 6 inches wide, and designed with bold colors, says: BRINGING CONTRABAND INTO THIS FACILITY IS A FELONY PUNISHABLE BY UP TO TWO YEARS IN PRISON. IF YOU HAVE CONTRABAND ON YOUR PERSON, DO NOT ENTER THIS FACILITY. IF YOU DO ENTER, YOU WILL BE SEARCHED, AND IF FOUND IN POSSESSION OF CONTRABAND, YOU WILL BE PUNISHED TO THE FULLEST EXTENT OF THE LAW.

At half of the state prisons, the size of the sign was increased to 36 inches tall and 18 inches wide. At the other prisons, no change to the sign was made. Otherwise, policies at all prisons were exactly the same—all visitors were searched, and all visitors possessing contraband were arrested and prosecuted. Here are the charts showing the number of contraband items discovered on visitors for the four quarters following the posting of the larger signs. Group A facilities had the new signage; Group B facilities had the old signage.

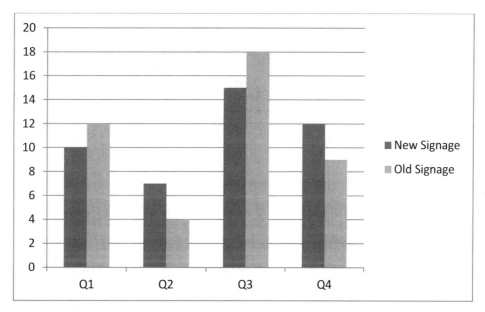

In which quarter was the difference between the two sets of facilities the greatest on a percentage basis?

    a. Q1
    b. Q2
    c. Q3
    d. Q4

10. There have been a string of armed robberies near a park over the past few weeks. Police believe most of them are the work of the same person. Here are suspect descriptions from the victim in each mugging.

Robbery	Height	Race	Age	Unique Identifiers
Robbery 1	6'0"	White	App. 30	Victim doesn't remember
Robbery 2	5'10"	White	Late 20s	Tattoo on left arm; possibly eagle
Robbery 3	6'2"	White	25-30	Possible tattoo on one arm
Robbery 4	5'7"	White	25-30	Large knife scar down left cheek

Which one of the robberies most likely wasn't committed by the same person?

    a.   1
    b.   2
    c.   3
    d.   4

11. This chart from the United States Department of Health and Human Services shows the percentage of people in each age bracket who have driven under the influence of alcohol at least once during the past 12 months.

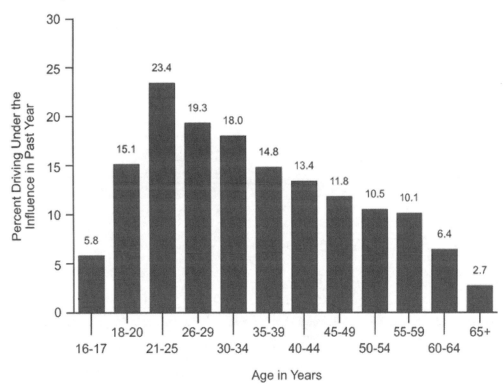

Which age bracket is third highest when it comes to the most people who have driven under the influence of alcohol in the past 12 months?

    a. 18-20
    b. 26-29
    c. 30-34
    d. 35-39

12. This chart from the United States Department of Health and Human Services shows the percentage of young people who reported that they had used alcohol in the past 30 days, broken down by age bracket and year.

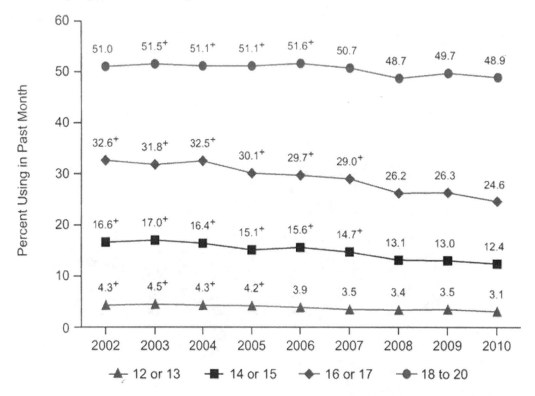

Which year had the highest percentage of 12–13-year-olds reporting alcohol use in the past 30 days?

    a. 2009
    b. 2006
    c. 2003
    d. 2005

13. Until recently, many local law enforcement agencies in one state required a minimum of an associate's degree for police academy recruits. After the state legislature passed a law setting new standards, all agencies in the state now require applicants to have a bachelor's degree (or higher). The number of recruits has plummeted. Here are the figures for four cities in the state. The first bar shows the number of applicants for the city's academy in 2012; the second bar is the number who applied in 2013.

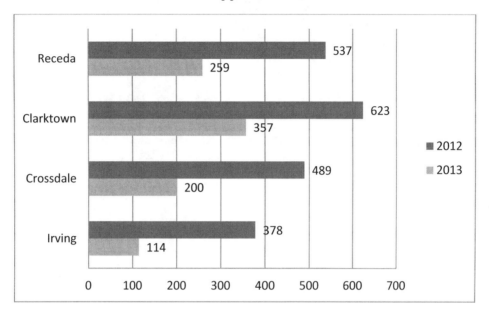

Which city experienced the greatest percentage decline in applicants in 2013?

    a. Irving
    b. Crossdale
    c. Clarktown
    d. Receda

14. This table shows the racial/ethnic breakdown of corrections officers at four facilities:

Facility	African American	Asian American	Hispanic	White
Milton	18%	2%	14%	66%
Ferguson	15%	2%	28%	55%
Dalton	32%	4%	30%	34%
Howard	12%	12%	24%	52%

Assuming each facility employs 200 officers, at which facility is the combined number of Asian-American and Hispanic officers equal to the number of white officers?

    a. Milton
    b. Ferguson
    c. Dalton
    d. Howard

15. Four correctional facilities recently held their annual physical exam for officers. Here is a table showing how many officers at each facility were told they need to lose weight, broken down by age range. Assuming each facility employs 50 officers in each age range, which facility has the most corrections officers that need to lose weight?

Facility	22-30	31-40	41-50	50+
Milton	6%	10%	4%	22%
Ferguson	20%	18%	22%	22%
Dalton	14%	10%	24%	30%
Howard	4%	6%	20%	36%

a. Milton
b. Ferguson
c. Dalton
d. Howard

Answer Key and Explanations

Written Comprehension

1. A: Officer Shantel Williams. The passage states that Jose Mendez punched a man who spilled a drink, and that the name of the man who spilled the drink was Roland Hemphill. It goes on to say that Officer Shantel Williams interviewed Hemphill. Officer Ronald Jones interviewed Mendez. Officer Mike Smith interviewed several witnesses who confirmed Hemphill's account. Officer Mark Jones interviewed the bartender, Tyreese Smith.

2. B: Two. Asia Campos was arrested on an outstanding warrant, and Ronald Holderman was arrested for the theft of the motorcycle from Orlando.

3. C: Seven items of contraband were found in the sweep — (1) a marijuana cigarette in Inmate Reggie Wilson's pillow, (2) a cup of homemade wine in Inmate Robert Doolittle's cell, (3) a mobile phone in the cell of Inmates Mustafa Johnson and Dewayne Smith, and (4, 5, 6 and 7) three syringes and a metal spoon in a cell shared by Inmates Ryan McDonald and Brent Travers.

4. C: Seven days. Ms. Snowden checked into the hotel on June 20. She was seen on June 22, but hasn't been seen since. The date of the officer's visit is June 29, which means seven days have passed since June 22, the last time anyone saw Ms. Snowden.

5. C: 5 feet 8 inches and 150 pounds. The tallest bank robber took off going east in a brown van, the second tallest went west on a motorcycle, the short, stocky one fled west in a white Honda Civic, and the other shorter robber drove west in a small pickup truck. There were two "shorter" robbers, each about 5 feet 8 inches. But one was stockier than the other, and he drove off in a white Honda Civic. That means the robber who was 5 feet 8 inches and 150 pounds is the one who fled in a pickup truck.

6. B: Two. Although Donte Broomfield threatened four people at the pay-per-view party and assaulted another person at another house before the party, the passage states that he physically assaulted two women at the pay-per-view party.

7. B: Crews and Mason. Corrections Officer Crews was assigned to Unit B for the first and third weeks, and Unit C for the second and fourth weeks. Corrections Officer Mason was assigned to Unit B for the first and third weeks, and Unit C for the second and fourth weeks.

8. D: Wellstone. Nesmith was seen stealing a hooded sweatshirt, Jackson is seen stealing women's cosmetics, Pierson was observed stealing candy, and Nesmith was seen on tape stuffing a dress down his pants.

9. A: Five. According to the neighbor, within the last six months, police officers had been to the house to investigate (1) public intoxication, (2) another time for a domestic dispute call, (3) a few weeks later for loud music, (4) then again for cars parking illegally and impeding traffic, and (5) the last time for a person who was drunk and disorderly.

10. D: The intersection of Eldridge and Scranton. The suspect turned east onto Eldridge Avenue, and then nearly caused a collision with another car at the intersection of Scranton Street.

11. D: Ethan Jones. The passage says that Ethan Jones, the son of Eric Jones, had a makeshift bandage around his head, which was stained with blood.

12. C: Gangster Disciples. Nine members of the Mexican Mafia were moved or transferred out, six members of the outlaws were moved or transferred out, nine members of the Latin Kings were moved or transferred out, and ten members of the Gangster Disciples were moved or transferred out.

13. C: Three. The first-time officers went to the scene, they apprehended two women, who were arrested. The second time, they detained five men and three women. Of the women, two were let go, and one was arrested. Added to the two arrested previously, that makes a total of three women arrested.

14. B: Caitlyn Malcolm. Britney Maddox, Rob Tellinger, and Ryan Tellinger were all passengers in the car driven by Caitlyn Malcolm, who was arrested for DUI.

15. D: Twelve. Friday night there were three arrests for selling drugs. Saturday afternoon there were two more. Late Saturday and early Sunday yielded seven more arrests for drug sales, for a total of twelve.

Written Expression

1. A: The word *depudy* should be spelled *deputy*. The other words are spelled correctly.

2. C: The correct word to use to fill in the blank is *described*. None of the other words make any sense in this sentence. *Describe* means to give an account, or to relate facts. *Subscribe* means to receive something on a regular basis, like a cable TV subscription. *Prescribe* means to recommend something, like a doctor's prescription. *Ascribe* means to say that something is caused by something else, as in "Steve ascribed his sore knees to too much jogging yesterday."

3. B: The word *arive* should be spelled *arrive*. The other words are spelled correctly.

4. C: *Must* is the only choice for filling in the blank that follows good grammar.

5. D. The word *cittizens* should be spelled *citizens*. The other words are spelled correctly.

6. A: The word *is* is the only choice for filling in the blank that follows good grammar.

7. A: The word *funural* should be spelled *funeral*. The other words are spelled correctly.

8. B: The word *assigned* is the only choice for filling in the blank that makes sense and follows good grammar.

9. B: The word *unpleasent* should be spelled *unpleasant*. The other words are spelled correctly.

10. D: The word *be* is the only choice for filling in the blank that follows good grammar.

11. C: The word *cheif* should be spelled *chief*. The other words are spelled correctly.

12. D: The phrase *be admitted to* is the only choice for filling in the blank that follows good grammar.

13. C: The word *steap* should be spelled *steep*. The other words are spelled correctly.

14. A: The phrase *have been* is the only choice for filling in the blank that follows good grammar.

15. C: The word *endorce* should be spelled *endorse*. The other words are spelled correctly.

Memorization

1. C: There are 14 people in the photo. There are 13 on or beside the stairs, and in the background, there is a woman with her back to the camera behind the man who is next to the stairs.

2. B: One person in the front row is wearing a dress.

3. B: One person is wearing glasses—the woman the dog is standing in front of.

4. D: The woman whose luggage the dog is sniffing is reading a book.

5. D: The officer on the right is taller.

6. C: The officer on the left is wearing sunglasses.

7. D: The officer on the right is in short sleeves.

8. C: The officer on the left is wearing a cap.

9. C: The officer on the left is wearing gloves.

10. B: The officer in the middle is tallest.

11. A: The officer on the left is holding his beverage in his right hand.

12. C: The street sign says 24th St

13. A: According to the mileage sign, Condon is 38 miles away.

14. A: The mileage sign is taller.

15. B: The arrow on the road sign is pointing left.

Deductive Reasoning

1. D: She will face no charges. She had $38,000 in money from drug deals in her possession. Because that is between $30,000 and $150,000, ordinarily it would qualify as a third-

Answer Key and Explanations

degree felony. However, she was on her way to turn the counterfeit money over to the closest law enforcement authority, the county sheriff. According to section (b) of the quoted portion of the criminal code, if a person has the money in their possession because they are acting with intent to facilitate the lawful seizure of illicit money, that is a defense from prosecution.

2. C: Quit the team immediately. Rule 29 says: "Associating or fraternizing with any person known to have been convicted of any felony or misdemeanor, either State or Federal, excluding traffic and municipal ordinance violations." It does not mention any exceptions, so the fact that your teammate has turned his life around in the five years since getting out of prison is meaningless as far as the rule is concerned, so *A* is wrong. Only associating with him at games still violates the rule, which doesn't allow for any fraternization or association, so *B* is incorrect. *D* is wrong because there's nothing to talk over with your supervisor, as the rule is clear and you should never ask for permission to break an official rule.

3. B: An inmate burning his arm with a lit cigarette. There is nothing in the information listed that would indicate that an inmate caught smoking a cigarette, smoking a joint, or possessing a cellphone would not be punished, so *A, C,* and *D* are all incorrect. However, (4) says that "commission of acts that should normally result in consideration for formal disciplinary action shall not be subject to such action when these acts are directly associated with an inmate's intentional self-injurious behavior," so even if it's violation of the rules for an inmate to possess a cigarette, the inmate should not be punished for trying to harm himself, but should instead receive the medical or psychological help he obviously needs.

4. B: (g). She would be in violation of the rule in (g) that says that hair dye must be a natural color. Since no humans have blue hair naturally, her blue highlights are forbidden. (f) is about neckties, so it isn't the right answer. (h) says that earrings are prohibited for male employees, but female employees are allowed to wear them. (j) is a broad rule about avoiding eccentricities and doesn't apply in this case.

5. A: While there are some rules that apply to children of different ages, (3) says "Visitors shall be required to register for visiting through the automated visiting record. The failure to do so or providing false information shall result in denial or termination of the visit and suspension of visiting privileges." Because no exceptions are listed, this applies to all child visitors, no matter their age.

6. D: Roman candles fall under the definition of illegal fireworks, while the text says that trick matches, party poppers, and toy guns are NOT classified as illegal fireworks.

7. B: The woman has committed a third-degree felony. It is very dangerous for children to be playing in the street, and it's even worse that they're doing so when they should be in bed, so the woman has clearly committed some form of child abuse. Misdemeanor child abuse is not listed as an option, so *A* is incorrect. Likewise, first-degree felony child abuse is also not mentioned, so *D* is wrong. It would be a second-degree felony if one or both of the children had suffered "great bodily harm, permanent disability, or permanent

disfigurement" as a result of their mother being negligent by letting them play in the street, but both children look healthy and have no injuries, so C is also incorrect.

8. C: A first-degree misdemeanor is treated as a third-degree felony. Gang-related offenses move up one degree from what the crime would be treated as if it weren't gang related. The next step up after a first-degree misdemeanor is a third-degree felony, as the text says.

9. B: Giving the man a warning about parking in handicapped parking spaces without a permit is not an acceptable response according to the guidelines, which state that the officer "shall" cite the driver for parking in a handicapped space without the required permit. So letting the driver off with a warning would be a violation of the guidelines. All three of the other answer choices would be acceptable. Note that the officer may, but isn't required to, have the car towed or charge the driver with resisting an officer without violence for not producing the permit. These two options are at the officer's discretion, but having the vehicle moved (by the driver or a city tow truck) and writing a ticket are both required actions.

10. A: The first thing you should do is call for an ambulance. If the other driver were bleeding, rendering first aid might be the first priority, but with no bleeding and no obvious injuries, there is little someone who isn't a medical professional can do, so B is wrong. However, the driver clearly needs medical attention, so you should call for an ambulance immediately. C is incorrect because calling for an ambulance is a much higher priority than calling for a supervisor to come to the scene. D is wrong because the text says that cars should be allowed to remain where they are except in emergency situations. So not only should you not move the vehicles before calling an ambulance, you shouldn't move them at all.

11. C: He should be charged with theft. Even though he entered the house with the intention of stealing something, he didn't commit burglary, because burglary is entering a building without permission for the purpose of committing a crime. The homeowners invited him in, so B is wrong. A is wrong for two reasons. One, he wasn't merely only the property; he stole something. Two, like burglary, criminal trespass only occurs when someone is on or in a property without permission, and he had permission to be in the house. And because he was invited in, and didn't force his way into an occupied dwelling, it wasn't a home invasion, so D is wrong.

12. A: He should be charged with criminal trespass. He didn't force his way in, and the house was empty, meaning it wasn't a home invasion, so D is incorrect. He didn't steal anything, so C (theft) is also incorrect. B is wrong because he didn't enter the home for the purpose of committing a crime, which is the definition of burglary.

13. D: They should be charged with home invasion and theft. The key here is that the house was occupied at the time, and they forced their way in for the purpose of committing the felony of threatening bodily harm to Steve, which constitutes assault. On top of that, they stole some tools, which is theft. It's not criminal trespass (A), because it was an occupied dwelling they broke into. It's not burglary (B), for the same reason. A person who breaks into an empty house and steals something is guilty of burglary, but a person who breaks

Answer Key and Explanations

121

into an occupied house and steals something is guilty of home invasion. Charging them with only theft (*C*) is insufficient, because it ignores the fact that they forced themselves into an occupied dwelling.

14. D: You should order the person using the foul language to leave the area or face arrest for disorderly conduct. The guidelines say that people should only be arrested for minor incidents as a last resort, and that you should strive to keep things from escalating. If you were only dealing with one person, and not with a large and angry crowd, an arrest for disorderly conduct would be appropriate. But with a large crowd of angry workers, an arrest might cause things to escalate, so *A* is wrong. B is wrong because you are not to offer your opinion about the dispute or take sides. *C* is incorrect for the same reason.

15. C: Make no arrests and call for backup, and when enough officers are on the scene arrest the worker for the property damage. *A* is incorrect, because, while it's true that you can't take sides in the dispute, you are required to enforce the law, and willfully damaging property is illegal. *B* is wrong, because the guidelines say to arrest the offender once enough officers are on the scene to control the situation. *D* is wrong because the crowd is large and hostile, and they are threatening that there will be trouble if you arrest the worker. To make an arrest before backup officers arrive would be putting yourself, your partner, and others in serious danger.

Inductive Reasoning

1. A: The bar with the lighter shading represents the data for the city that didn't pass the law. For each year, the first bar shows the percentage of victims who *refused* to testify. The question is asking you to determine in which two years the highest percentage of victims *agreed* to testify. This is the opposite of what the graph shows, so instead of looking for the tallest two bars in this category, you need to find the shortest two bars. In the category of victims who refused to testify in the city that didn't pass the law, the two shortest bars are in 2005 and 2007. In 2005, 25% of victims refused to testify, so 75% agreed to testify. In 2007, 15% of victims refused to testify, meaning 85% agreed to testify.

2. D: This is a very basic pie chart, and it doesn't just shade each portion of the chart, but also includes the percentages. To answer this question, you simply need to find the month with the biggest number on the chart, which is December, at 17%.

3. D: In 2013, there were a little over 2000 robberies, while there were well under 2000 auto thefts. For every other year, the number of auto thefts is higher than the number of robberies.

4. A: Only two categories increased from 2011 to 2014. The biggest category, *Non-family*, decreased from 56% to 46%. *Other Family* stayed the same at 18%. The category of abusers in the *Parent* category increased from 14% to 16%, while Spouse/Partner saw an increase from 12% to 20%.

5. A: Of the five categories represented in the pie charts, only one shows the same percentage in both 2010 and 2011—Asia, at 15%.

6. B: An intersection must have a number of 1.25 or higher in the Red-Light Runners Column, *and* a number of 1.10 or higher in the Red-Light Running Accidents Column. Intersections 2, 4, and 6 all have 1.25 or higher in the Red-Light Runners Column, but 2 only has 1.00 in the Red-Light Running Accidents Column. Only intersections 4 and 6 meet both criteria—.

7. C: To answer this question, you'll need to do some math. First, convert the average times into seconds. There are sixty seconds in a minute, so 10:07 becomes 607 seconds, 9:40 is 580, 9:37 is 577, and 9:46 is 586. Adding these together gives you 2350 seconds. Divide by four to get the average, which is 587.5. Then divide 587.5 by 60 to convert it back into minutes, which produces 9, with a remainder of 47.5. So the average response time for the patrol cars in the trial was 9:47.5 seconds. This is 12.5 seconds lower than the benchmark of 10:00.

8. D: June and August both had 12 accidents. None of the other pairs had the same number of accidents. January had 10 and September had 9, making *A* wrong. February had 11 and June had 10, so *B* is wrong. May had 8 and November had 5, so *C* is incorrect.

9. B: To find the percentage difference, subtract the lower number from the higher number, and divide the result by the higher number. So in Q1 subtract 12-10 leaves 2. 2/12 is .1666, or around 17%. In other words, there were 17% more contraband items discovered at one facility than at the other for Q1. For Q3, the difference was also about 17%, while in Q4 the difference was 33%. In Q2, however, the difference was 75%.

10. D: While no two of the descriptions are exactly the same, the first three are similar enough that it's very likely they're describing the same person. In all three the suspect is white, and all three of the first victims said he is six feet tall or within a couple inches of six feet. Two of the victims say he had or might have had a tattoo on one of his arms, while the first victim doesn't remember. They all place him in about the same age range, from 25-30, although expressed in different ways. In the fourth robbery, the suspect shares the age and race of the suspect in the other three robberies, but he's described as being nearly half a foot shorter than six feet tall, and he also has a large scar on his face. It's very unlikely that this is the same suspect as in the other three muggings, because it's difficult to believe the other three victims wouldn't have noticed the scar, or would have overestimated the suspect's height so badly.

11. C: The question was which age bracket was third highest. The age bracket of 21-25 has the highest percentage of people who have driven under the influence of alcohol in the past 12 months, 23.4%. Second highest is 26-29, at 19.3%. The third highest is 30-34, at 18.0%.

12. C: The green line at the bottom of the chart represents 12- and 13-year-olds who reported that they had used alcohol in the past 30 days, and the triangle marks the year. In 2003, 4.5+% of 12- and 13-year-olds reported using alcohol in the past 30 days, and 4.5+ is the highest number on that line.

13. A: To answer this question, you can use the same formula used to answer Question 9. To find the percentage difference, subtract the lower number from the higher number, and divide the result by the higher number. Doing so will show that Irving had the greatest percentage drop of all four cities. However, it's really not necessary to do any math to find the answer. You can compare the 2012 bar to the 2013 bar with a quick glance, and see that the decrease appears to be the biggest on the city of Irving's bars, proportionally.

14. C: At Dalton, 34% of officers are white. Asian-Americans make up 4% of the staff, and Hispanics are 30%, equaling 34%.

15. B: Ferguson. Add up the percentages of officers in each age range. The facility with the highest total percentage is the facility with the greatest number of officers that need to lose weight. 44% of Milton officers, 82% of Ferguson officers, 78% of Dalton officers, and 66% of Howard officers need to lose weight.

PHOTO CREDITS

All photos licensed under CC BY 4.0 (creativecommons.org/licenses/by/4.0/)

Example Photo: "zany booth 05" by peteandcharlotte (www.flickr.com/photos/90784784@N08/8269117136)

Photo 1: "people" by Vladimir Pustovit (www.flickr.com/photos/pustovit/14561150953)

Photo 2: "The Harbor Police K-9 Team" by Port of San Diego (www.flickr.com/photos/portofsandiego/7157651521)

Photo 3: "115.WeCanEndAIDS.WhiteHouse.WDC.24July2012" by Elvert Barnes (www.flickr.com/photos/95413346@N00/7641811310)

Photo 4: "police officers and the carnaval in the mission : san Francisco" by torbakhopper (www.flickr.com/photos/32029534@N00/14083609378)

Photo 5: "Oregon Route 19" by Curtis Perry (www.flickr.com/photos/33124677@N00/25373305973)

How to Overcome Test Anxiety

Just the thought of taking a test is enough to make most people a little nervous. A test is an important event that can have a long-term impact on your future, so it's important to take it seriously and it's natural to feel anxious about performing well. But just because anxiety is normal, that doesn't mean that it's helpful in test taking, or that you should simply accept it as part of your life. Anxiety can have a variety of effects. These effects can be mild, like making you feel slightly nervous, or severe, like blocking your ability to focus or remember even a simple detail.

If you experience test anxiety—whether severe or mild—it's important to know how to beat it. To discover this, first you need to understand what causes test anxiety.

Causes of Test Anxiety

While we often think of anxiety as an uncontrollable emotional state, it can actually be caused by simple, practical things. One of the most common causes of test anxiety is that a person does not feel adequately prepared for their test. This feeling can be the result of many different issues such as poor study habits or lack of organization, but the most common culprit is time management. Starting to study too late, failing to organize your study time to cover all of the material, or being distracted while you study will mean that you're not well prepared for the test. This may lead to cramming the night before, which will cause you to be physically and mentally exhausted for the test. Poor time management also contributes to feelings of stress, fear, and hopelessness as you realize you are not well prepared but don't know what to do about it.

Other times, test anxiety is not related to your preparation for the test but comes from unresolved fear. This may be a past failure on a test, or poor performance on tests in general. It may come from comparing yourself to others who seem to be performing better or from the stress of living up to expectations. Anxiety may be driven by fears of the future—how failure on this test would affect your educational and career goals. These fears are often completely irrational, but they can still negatively impact your test performance.

Elements of Test Anxiety

As mentioned earlier, test anxiety is considered to be an emotional state, but it has physical and mental components as well. Sometimes you may not even realize that you are suffering from test anxiety until you notice the physical symptoms. These can include trembling hands, rapid heartbeat, sweating, nausea, and tense muscles. Extreme anxiety may lead to fainting or vomiting. Obviously, any of these symptoms can have a negative impact on testing. It is important to recognize them as soon as they begin to occur so that you can address the problem before it damages your performance.

The mental components of test anxiety include trouble focusing and inability to remember learned information. During a test, your mind is on high alert, which can help you recall information and stay focused for an extended period of time. However, anxiety interferes

125

with your mind's natural processes, causing you to blank out, even on the questions you know well. The strain of testing during anxiety makes it difficult to stay focused, especially on a test that may take several hours. Extreme anxiety can take a huge mental toll, making it difficult not only to recall test information but even to understand the test questions or pull your thoughts together.

Effects of Test Anxiety

Test anxiety is like a disease—if left untreated, it will get progressively worse. Anxiety leads to poor performance, and this reinforces the feelings of fear and failure, which in turn lead to poor performances on subsequent tests. It can grow from a mild nervousness to a crippling condition. If allowed to progress, test anxiety can have a big impact on your schooling, and consequently on your future.

Test anxiety can spread to other parts of your life. Anxiety on tests can become anxiety in any stressful situation, and blanking on a test can turn into panicking in a job situation. But fortunately, you don't have to let anxiety rule your testing and determine your grades. There are a number of relatively simple steps you can take to move past anxiety and function normally on a test and in the rest of life.

Physical Steps for Beating Test Anxiety

While test anxiety is a serious problem, the good news is that it can be overcome. It doesn't have to control your ability to think and remember information. While it may take time, you can begin taking steps today to beat anxiety.

Just as your first hint that you may be struggling with anxiety comes from the physical symptoms, the first step to treating it is also physical. Rest is crucial for having a clear, strong mind. If you are tired, it is much easier to give in to anxiety. But if you establish good sleep habits, your body and mind will be ready to perform optimally, without the strain of exhaustion. Additionally, sleeping well helps you to retain information better, so you're more likely to recall the answers when you see the test questions.

Getting good sleep means more than going to bed on time. It's important to allow your brain time to relax. Take study breaks from time to time so it doesn't get overworked, and don't study right before bed. Take time to rest your mind before trying to rest your body, or you may find it difficult to fall asleep.

Along with sleep, other aspects of physical health are important in preparing for a test. Good nutrition is vital for good brain function. Sugary foods and drinks may give a burst of energy but this burst is followed by a crash, both physically and emotionally. Instead, fuel your body with protein and vitamin-rich foods.

Also, drink plenty of water. Dehydration can lead to headaches and exhaustion, especially if your brain is already under stress from the rigors of the test. Particularly if your test is a long one, drink water during the breaks. And if possible, take an energy-boosting snack to eat between sections.

Along with sleep and diet, a third important part of physical health is exercise. Maintaining a steady workout schedule is helpful, but even taking 5-minute study breaks to walk can help get your blood pumping faster and clear your head. Exercise also releases endorphins, which contribute to a positive feeling and can help combat test anxiety.

When you nurture your physical health, you are also contributing to your mental health. If your body is healthy, your mind is much more likely to be healthy as well. So take time to rest, nourish your body with healthy food and water, and get moving as much as possible. Taking these physical steps will make you stronger and more able to take the mental steps necessary to overcome test anxiety.

Mental Steps for Beating Test Anxiety

Working on the mental side of test anxiety can be more challenging, but as with the physical side, there are clear steps you can take to overcome it. As mentioned earlier, test anxiety often stems from lack of preparation, so the obvious solution is to prepare for the test. Effective studying may be the most important weapon you have for beating test anxiety, but you can and should employ several other mental tools to combat fear.

First, boost your confidence by reminding yourself of past success—tests or projects that you aced. If you're putting as much effort into preparing for this test as you did for those, there's no reason you should expect to fail here. Work hard to prepare; then trust your preparation.

Second, surround yourself with encouraging people. It can be helpful to find a study group, but be sure that the people you're around will encourage a positive attitude. If you spend time with others who are anxious or cynical, this will only contribute to your own anxiety. Look for others who are motivated to study hard from a desire to succeed, not from a fear of failure.

Third, reward yourself. A test is physically and mentally tiring, even without anxiety, and it can be helpful to have something to look forward to. Plan an activity following the test, regardless of the outcome, such as going to a movie or getting ice cream.

When you are taking the test, if you find yourself beginning to feel anxious, remind yourself that you know the material. Visualize successfully completing the test. Then take a few deep, relaxing breaths and return to it. Work through the questions carefully but with confidence, knowing that you are capable of succeeding.

Developing a healthy mental approach to test taking will also aid in other areas of life. Test anxiety affects more than just the actual test—it can be damaging to your mental health and even contribute to depression. It's important to beat test anxiety before it becomes a problem for more than testing.

Study Strategy

Being prepared for the test is necessary to combat anxiety, but what does being prepared look like? You may study for hours on end and still not feel prepared. What you need is a

How to Overcome Test Anxiety

strategy for test prep. The next few pages outline our recommended steps to help you plan out and conquer the challenge of preparation.

STEP 1: SCOPE OUT THE TEST

Learn everything you can about the format (multiple choice, essay, etc.) and what will be on the test. Gather any study materials, course outlines, or sample exams that may be available. Not only will this help you to prepare, but knowing what to expect can help to alleviate test anxiety.

STEP 2: MAP OUT THE MATERIAL

Look through the textbook or study guide and make note of how many chapters or sections it has. Then divide these over the time you have. For example, if a book has 15 chapters and you have five days to study, you need to cover three chapters each day. Even better, if you have the time, leave an extra day at the end for overall review after you have gone through the material in depth.

If time is limited, you may need to prioritize the material. Look through it and make note of which sections you think you already have a good grasp on, and which need review. While you are studying, skim quickly through the familiar sections and take more time on the challenging parts. Write out your plan so you don't get lost as you go. Having a written plan also helps you feel more in control of the study, so anxiety is less likely to arise from feeling overwhelmed at the amount to cover.

STEP 3: GATHER YOUR TOOLS

Decide what study method works best for you. Do you prefer to highlight in the book as you study and then go back over the highlighted portions? Or do you type out notes of the important information? Or is it helpful to make flashcards that you can carry with you? Assemble the pens, index cards, highlighters, post-it notes, and any other materials you may need so you won't be distracted by getting up to find things while you study.

If you're having a hard time retaining the information or organizing your notes, experiment with different methods. For example, try color-coding by subject with colored pens, highlighters, or post-it notes. If you learn better by hearing, try recording yourself reading your notes so you can listen while in the car, working out, or simply sitting at your desk. Ask a friend to quiz you from your flashcards, or try teaching someone the material to solidify it in your mind.

STEP 4: CREATE YOUR ENVIRONMENT

It's important to avoid distractions while you study. This includes both the obvious distractions like visitors and the subtle distractions like an uncomfortable chair (or a too-comfortable couch that makes you want to fall asleep). Set up the best study environment possible: good lighting and a comfortable work area. If background music helps you focus, you may want to turn it on, but otherwise keep the room quiet. If you are using a computer to take notes, be sure you don't have any other windows open, especially applications like social media, games, or anything else that could distract you. Silence your phone and turn off notifications. Be sure to keep water close by so you stay hydrated while you study (but avoid unhealthy drinks and snacks).

Also, take into account the best time of day to study. Are you freshest first thing in the morning? Try to set aside some time then to work through the material. Is your mind clearer in the afternoon or evening? Schedule your study session then. Another method is to study at the same time of day that you will take the test, so that your brain gets used to working on the material at that time and will be ready to focus at test time.

STEP 5: STUDY!

Once you have done all the study preparation, it's time to settle into the actual studying. Sit down, take a few moments to settle your mind so you can focus, and begin to follow your study plan. Don't give in to distractions or let yourself procrastinate. This is your time to prepare so you'll be ready to fearlessly approach the test. Make the most of the time and stay focused.

Of course, you don't want to burn out. If you study too long you may find that you're not retaining the information very well. Take regular study breaks. For example, taking five minutes out of every hour to walk briskly, breathing deeply and swinging your arms, can help your mind stay fresh.

As you get to the end of each chapter or section, it's a good idea to do a quick review. Remind yourself of what you learned and work on any difficult parts. When you feel that you've mastered the material, move on to the next part. At the end of your study session, briefly skim through your notes again.

But while review is helpful, cramming last minute is NOT. If at all possible, work ahead so that you won't need to fit all your study into the last day. Cramming overloads your brain with more information than it can process and retain, and your tired mind may struggle to recall even previously learned information when it is overwhelmed with last-minute study. Also, the urgent nature of cramming and the stress placed on your brain contribute to anxiety. You'll be more likely to go to the test feeling unprepared and having trouble thinking clearly.

So don't cram, and don't stay up late before the test, even just to review your notes at a leisurely pace. Your brain needs rest more than it needs to go over the information again. In fact, plan to finish your studies by noon or early afternoon the day before the test. Give your brain the rest of the day to relax or focus on other things, and get a good night's sleep. Then you will be fresh for the test and better able to recall what you've studied.

STEP 6: TAKE A PRACTICE TEST

Many courses offer sample tests, either online or in the study materials. This is an excellent resource to check whether you have mastered the material, as well as to prepare for the test format and environment.

Check the test format ahead of time: the number of questions, the type (multiple choice, free response, etc.), and the time limit. Then create a plan for working through them. For example, if you have 30 minutes to take a 60-question test, your limit is 30 seconds per question. Spend less time on the questions you know well so that you can take more time on the difficult ones.

How to Overcome Test Anxiety

If you have time to take several practice tests, take the first one open book, with no time limit. Work through the questions at your own pace and make sure you fully understand them. Gradually work up to taking a test under test conditions: sit at a desk with all study materials put away and set a timer. Pace yourself to make sure you finish the test with time to spare and go back to check your answers if you have time.

After each test, check your answers. On the questions you missed, be sure you understand why you missed them. Did you misread the question (tests can use tricky wording)? Did you forget the information? Or was it something you hadn't learned? Go back and study any shaky areas that the practice tests reveal.

Taking these tests not only helps with your grade, but also aids in combating test anxiety. If you're already used to the test conditions, you're less likely to worry about it, and working through tests until you're scoring well gives you a confidence boost. Go through the practice tests until you feel comfortable, and then you can go into the test knowing that you're ready for it.

Test Tips

On test day, you should be confident, knowing that you've prepared well and are ready to answer the questions. But aside from preparation, there are several test day strategies you can employ to maximize your performance.

First, as stated before, get a good night's sleep the night before the test (and for several nights before that, if possible). Go into the test with a fresh, alert mind rather than staying up late to study.

Try not to change too much about your normal routine on the day of the test. It's important to eat a nutritious breakfast, but if you normally don't eat breakfast at all, consider eating just a protein bar. If you're a coffee drinker, go ahead and have your normal coffee. Just make sure you time it so that the caffeine doesn't wear off right in the middle of your test. Avoid sugary beverages, and drink enough water to stay hydrated but not so much that you need a restroom break 10 minutes into the test. If your test isn't first thing in the morning, consider going for a walk or doing a light workout before the test to get your blood flowing.

Allow yourself enough time to get ready, and leave for the test with plenty of time to spare so you won't have the anxiety of scrambling to arrive in time. Another reason to be early is to select a good seat. It's helpful to sit away from doors and windows, which can be distracting. Find a good seat, get out your supplies, and settle your mind before the test begins.

When the test begins, start by going over the instructions carefully, even if you already know what to expect. Make sure you avoid any careless mistakes by following the directions.

Then begin working through the questions, pacing yourself as you've practiced. If you're not sure on an answer, don't spend too much time on it, and don't let it shake your confidence. Either skip it and come back later, or eliminate as many wrong answers as possible and guess among the remaining ones. Don't dwell on these questions as you continue—put them out of your mind and focus on what lies ahead.

Be sure to read all of the answer choices, even if you're sure the first one is the right answer. Sometimes you'll find a better one if you keep reading. But don't second-guess yourself if you do immediately know the answer. Your gut instinct is usually right. Don't let test anxiety rob you of the information you know.

If you have time at the end of the test (and if the test format allows), go back and review your answers. Be cautious about changing any, since your first instinct tends to be correct, but make sure you didn't misread any of the questions or accidentally mark the wrong answer choice. Look over any you skipped and make an educated guess.

At the end, leave the test feeling confident. You've done your best, so don't waste time worrying about your performance or wishing you could change anything. Instead, celebrate the successful completion of this test. And finally, use this test to learn how to deal with anxiety even better next time.

> **Review Video: Test Anxiety**
> Visit mometrix.com/academy and enter code: 100340

Important Qualification

Not all anxiety is created equal. If your test anxiety is causing major issues in your life beyond the classroom or testing center, or if you are experiencing troubling physical symptoms related to your anxiety, it may be a sign of a serious physiological or psychological condition. If this sounds like your situation, we strongly encourage you to seek professional help.

How to Overcome Test Anxiety

Additional Bonus Material

Due to our efforts to try to keep this book to a manageable length, we've created a link that will give you access to all of your additional bonus material:

mometrix.com/bonus948/cjbat